The Contras,
1980–1989

THE WASHINGTON PAPERS

. . . intended to meet the need for an authoritative, yet prompt, public appraisal of the major developments in world affairs.

President, CSIS: David M. Abshire

Series Editor: Walter Laqueur

Director of Publications: Nancy B. Eddy

Managing Editor: Donna R. Spitler

MANUSCRIPT SUBMISSION

The Washington Papers and Praeger Publishers welcome inquiries concerning manuscript submissions. Please include with your inquiry a curriculum vitae, synopsis, table of contents, and estimated manuscript length. Manuscripts must be between 120–200 double-spaced typed pages. All submissions will be peer reviewed. Submissions to *The Washington Papers* should be sent to *The Washington Papers*; The Center for Strategic and International Studies; 1800 K Street NW; Suite 400; Washington, DC 20006. Book proposals should be sent to Praeger Publishers; One Madison Avenue; New York NY 10010.

The Contras, 1980–1989

A Special Kind of Politics

R. Pardo-Maurer

Foreword by Edward N. Luttwak

Published with The Center for
Strategic and International Studies
Washington, D.C.

New York
Westport, Connecticut
London

Library of Congress Cataloging-in-Publication Data

Pardo-Maurer, R. (Rogelio)
  The Contras, 1980–1989 : a special kind of politics / R. Pardo-
Maurer : foreword by Edward N. Luttwak.
      p.   cm. – (The Washington papers, ISSN 0278-937X : 147)
  "Published with the Center for Strategic and International
Studies, Washington, D.C."
  Includes bibliographical references (p.   ) and index.
  ISBN 0-275-93817-4 (HB). – ISBN 0-275-93818-2 (PB)
  1. Nicaragua – Politics and government – 1979-
2. Counterrevolutionaries – Nicaragua – History – 20th century.
3. Government, Resistance to – Nicaragua – History – 20th century.
4. Nicaragua – Relations – United States.   5. United States –
Relations – Nicaragua.   I. Center for Strategic and International
Studies (Washington, D.C.)   II. Title.   III. Series.
F1528.P32   1990
972.8505'3 – dc20   90-44608

British Library Cataloging-in-Publication data is available.

Library of Congress Catalog Card Number: 90-44608
ISBN: 0-275-93817-4 (cloth)
        0-275-93818-2 (paper)

First published in 1990

Praeger Publishers, One Madison Avenue, New York, NY 10010
An imprint of Greenwood Publishing Group, Inc.

Printed in the United States of America

∞
The paper used in this book complies with the Permanent
Paper Standard issued by the National Information Standards
Organization (Z39.48-1984).

10   9   8   7   6   5   4   3   2   1

To the friends and mentors
who made history alive for me:
Sir Steven Runciman, Sir Harry Hinsley,
and Henry Ashby Turner

Contents

Foreword   ix

About the Author   xiii

Principal Abbreviations   xv

Principal Persons Mentioned   xvii

Summary   xxi

1. Introduction: The Early Years, 1980–1985   1

2. 1985: The Ideal Resistance   7

3. 1986: The Real Resistance   46

4. 1987: A Fresh Start   71

5. 1988: A False Start   96

Postscript   125

Appendix: Chronology of Events   133

Notes   135

Index   147

Foreword

The reader of this examination of the internal and external politics of the Nicaraguan opposition-in-arms, the contras, is in for several surprises. First, the author combines an unfailingly rigorous analysis that satisfies all the normal criteria of scholarship with narrative skills of a high order. The division of the text into short segments each headed by a concise summary in the old novelistic style is an elegant device that works very well within the compass of this work, keeping the reader on track through complicated events. The language, too, is far different in texture and tone from the standard academic norm. The contra experience was replete with conflictual tensions and factional intrigue, and the author would have slighted both had he not been bold enough to adopt a frankly dramatic manner. The result is a text that even readers not especially interested in Nicaraguan affairs will find most attractive.

Second, this study of the peculiar politics of exiles succeeds very well as a study of politics as such and could indeed serve as something of a model. What others too often dysfunctionally isolate is here found successfully combined: personalities and personality conflicts as well as elective affinities, ideology as both a genuine frame of reference and as the vehicle of symbols and themes apt to be manipulated by contending personalities and factions, and the organizational dimension. That politics is none of these things alone but rather precisely their combination is known to all. Yet their fusion into one many-layered account is far less common in the contemporary writings of political science than their arbitrary separation. In particular, it is not only historicists who are reluctant to contend with the role of personalities in politics, refractory as they are to systematic analysis. In this case, it would have been most misleading to record in merely procedural fashion the doings and undoings of the likes of Adolfo Calero and Oliver North.

Third, the author combines the intimate knowledge of an active participant with a dispassionate objectivity that is everywhere confirmed. That most unusual pairing of attributes is especially valuable in this case, for the contras and their American patrons were of course operating in secrecy, and only a participant could know of sayings and doings not otherwise recorded in the documentary evidence. Incidentally, the author's coldly disengaged manner only adds force to his observations on the role of U.S. policy and U.S. officials in the travails of the contras. It is with a devastating detachment that frivolous congressional reversals, irresponsible executive vacillations, and the disastrous operational incompetence of the CIA are noted at each remove.

Central America is both very near to the United States and very remote from its political culture. That the region's travails are of importance simply because they powerfully manifest themselves in our everyday life is by now a cliché. Yet any real knowledge of Central America and of its politics remains something of a rarity in the United States, so that many of our dealings with Central Americans and their lands are distorted by a profound ignorance unaccompanied by the modicum of humility that attends our dealings with more distant cultures. That is why the most outlandish notions of our own making have been projected onto Central American events during the past decade. One sustained example is the Vietnam-inspired perspective so often imposed on El Salvador's war. Another is the persistent misperception if not misrepresentation of the Nicaraguan resistance as a mere artifact of the CIA. R. Pardo-Maurer's account reveals the complex realities of the Nicaraguan resistance as an autonomous political phenomenon, though one both promoted and undermined by incoherent U.S. actions. This valuable contribution to our understanding of an important episode in the history of Central America deserves our close attention, if only as a corrective to delusions of adequacy engendered by both ignorance and arrogance.

Edward N. Luttwak
The Arleigh Burke Chair in Strategy
The Center for Strategic and International Studies

September 1990

About the Author

R. Pardo-Maurer joined the contras as a political officer in 1986, serving as special assistant to the Washington Office of the Nicaraguan Resistance until the Sapoa cease-fire of 1988. A national of both Costa Rica and the United States, he currently works at the American Enterprise Institute in Washington, D.C. Mr. Pardo-Maurer holds degrees from Yale and King's College, Cambridge.

Principal Abbreviations

Contras

ARDE—Alianza Revolucionaria Democrática
BOS—Bloque Opositor del Sur
FARN—Fuerzas Armadas Revolucionarias Nicaragüenses
FDN—Fuerza Democrática Nicaragüense
FRS—Frente Revolucionario Sandino
MILPAS—Milicias Populares Anti-Sandinistas (Anti-Somocistas before 1980)
RN—Resistencia Nicaragüense
UNO—Unidad Nicaragüense Opositora

Indian Revolt

KISAN—Kus Indian Sut Asla Nicaragua ra
MISURA—Miskito, Sumo, Rama
YATAMA—Yapti Tasba Masraka Aslika Takanka

Sandinistas

BLI—Batallon de Lucha Irregular (Irregular Combat Battalion)
EPS—Ejército Popular Sandinista (Sandinista Army)
FLSN—Frente Sandinista de Liberación Nacional
GPP—Guerra Popular Prolongada (Prolonged Popular War—Tomás Borge's faction)

Principal Persons Mentioned

Directors of Unidad Nicaragüense Opositora (UNO) or the Nicaraguan Resistance (the Contras) (Dates of participation in the resistance in parentheses)

Adolfo CALERO Portocarrero (1982–1989): Chairman of Milca bottling company; leader of the Conservative Party; member of the Broad Opposition Front against Somoza, 1978–1979

Alfredo CESAR Aguirre (1984–1989): General administrator of San Antonio sugar mill; secretary of the Sandinista junta, 1979; president of Central Bank (1980–1982)

Pedro Joaquin CHAMORRO Barrios (1987–1988): Journalist; coeditor of *La Prensa*, 1981–1984; political secretary of Social Democratic Party, 1983

Arturo CRUZ, Sr. (1985–1987): President of Central Bank, 1979–1980; member of Sandinista junta, 1980–1981; ambassador to Washington, 1981; presidential candidate, 1984

Azucena FERREY Echaverry (1987–1988): Student activist, Christian Democrat Party; vice president of the

Social Christian Party, 1983; general secretary, Women's Social Christian Union, 1985

Roberto FERREY Echaverry (1988–present): Lawyer with Ministry of Justice under the Frente Sandinista de Liberación Nacional (FSLN), 1979–1983; member of Alianza Revolucionaria Democrática (ARDE), 1983; secretary of the Resistance Directorate, 1987

Wilfredo MONTALVAN Duarte (1988–present): Journalist; Social Democratic Party activist

Alfonso ROBELO Callejas (1985–1988): President of Chamber of Commerce until 1975; cofounder of Nicaraguan Democratic Movement, 1978; leader of the Broad Opposition Front, 1978–1979; member of the Sandinista junta, 1979–1980; cofounder of ARDE, 1982

Aristides SANCHEZ Herdocia (1980–present): Cattle-rancher; exiled 1980; cofounder of the Fuerza Democrática Nicaragüense (FDN); FDN general secretary, 1983

Commanders of the Principal War Fronts

Enrique BERMUDEZ Varela ("Comandante 380"): Mathematics instructor; National Guard colonel; military attaché in Washington, D.C., 1975–1979; commander of the northern front

Fernando CHAMORRO Rappaccioli ("El Negro"): Leader of guerrilla takeover of Diriamba barracks, 1960; jailed after bazooka attacks on Somoza's bunker and ransomed by Pastora, 1978; veteran of Southern Front, 1978–1979; exiled 1981

Eden PASTORA Gomez ("Comandante Cero"): Conservative Party activist; joined FSLN for Pancasan guerrilla campaign, 1967; leader of FSLN capture of National Palace, 1978; commander of Southern Front in war against Somoza

Resistance (Contra) Officials

Leonardo SOMARRIBA Gonzalez: Secretary general/financial comptroller

Ernesto PALAZIO Hurtado: Representative in Washington for UNO/Resistencia Nicaragüense (RN)

Bosco MATAMOROS Hueck: FDN representative in Washington/resistance military spokesman

Donald CASTILLO Rivas: Secretary of international relations

U.S. Officials

Elliott Abrams: Assistant secretary of state for inter-American affairs, 1985–1989

Frank Carlucci: National security adviser, 1986–1987

Robert McFarlane: National security adviser, 1983–1985

Langhorne Motley: Assistant secretary of state for inter-American affairs, 1983–1985

Constantine Menges: Special assistant to the president for national security (Latin America), 1983–1985

John Negroponte: Special assistant to the president for national security (Latin America), 1987–1989

Lt. Col. Oliver North: Deputy director for political/military affairs, National Security Council, 1983–1986

Rear Admiral John Poindexter: National security adviser, 1985–1986

José Sorzano: Special assistant to the president for national security (Latin America), 1986–1987

U.S. Congress

Members, House of Representatives

Thomas ("Tip") O'Neill, Jr. (D-Mass.): Speaker, 1977–1986

James C. Wright, Jr. (D-Tex.): Speaker, 1987–1989

Robert Michel (R-Ill.): Minority Leader

Edward Boland (D-Mass.)

Dave McCurdy (D-Okla.)

Mickey Edwards (R-Okla.)

Jack Kemp (R-N.Y.)

Senators

Robert C. Byrd (D-W.Va.): Senate Majority Leader

Robert Dole (R-Kans.): Senate Minority Leader

Sandinista Officials

Daniel ORTEGA Saavedra: President of Nicaragua

Humberto ORTEGA Saavedra: Defense minister

Joaquin CUADRA Lacayo: Sandinista chief-of-staff

Roger MIRANDA Bengoechea: Chief of Defense Ministry Secretariat

Victor HUGO Tinoco: Vice foreign minister

Others

Oscar ARIAS Sanchez: President of Costa Rica

José AZCONA Hoyo: President of Honduras

Miguel Cardinal OBANDO y Bravo: Primate of Nicaragua

Summary

The exposure of Lt. Col. Oliver North's private supply network fractured the fragile internal equilibrium the contras had attained between 1985 and 1986 and threatened to crush the movement in America's intestine debate. Yet at the same time emerged powerful incentives for unity. Nicaragua became a desperate place, as Sandinista repression reached a crux. Congress released $100 million in aid to the resistance: if political and military successes could be scored, more was likely to follow. At the same time, the diplomatic process initiated by President Arias of Costa Rica placed upon the resistance hitherto unthinkable demands for political discipline.

Thus a bewildering array of forces jarred into motion, which from 1987 onward kept the leadership of the contras in a state of tumult. From the confusion emerged an intelligent amalgam of political and military objectives that made possible such steps as the chartering of a unified Nicaraguan Resistance, acceptance of the Arias plan, alliances with the internal opposition, and the negotiation of a cease-fire linked to democratization measures.

In such a highly charged atmosphere, the political fortunes of the individual directors of the resistance reflected the unsettling influence of events. From impregnable chief of the movement in 1986, Adolfo Calero was depressed to little more than decorative functions by the time of the signing of the cease-fire at Sapoa. His slide was immediately traceable to the breakup of North's supply ring. From the headship of an obscure leftist tendency, Alfredo Cesar became the preeminent political tactician of the resistance, emerging *pari passu* as the House of Representatives affirmed its prime authority on the Nicaragua question.

The leaders of the resistance found that influences external to the movement were to be calculated with as much delicacy as the many, often conflicting claims pressed by its members. Middle-class Nicaraguans, plundered peasants and merchants, persecuted evangelists, rich exiles, disillusioned Trotskyites, and Miskito Indians stood cheek-by-jowl with Reagan Republicans and Truman Democrats, not to mention State, Defense, and the CIA. Such awkward coalitions were predisposed to faction and intrigue. Quite naturally the movement's leaders assumed a polymorphous and defensive cast. This in turn left the resistance vulnerable to charges of tactical ineptitude and lackluster vision.

This book tells why. It provides a historical account of the choices and forces shaping the Nicaraguan Resistance up to the signing of the cease-fire at Sapoa, the period in which the author served as political assistant to the representative of the resistance in Washington. Special attention is devoted to the influence of the American political process on resistance strategy. The author fills in the map of the main factions and issues, leading to the stark conclusion that it was the men at the top who made the ultimate difference to the fate of the movement.

The Contras,
1980–1989

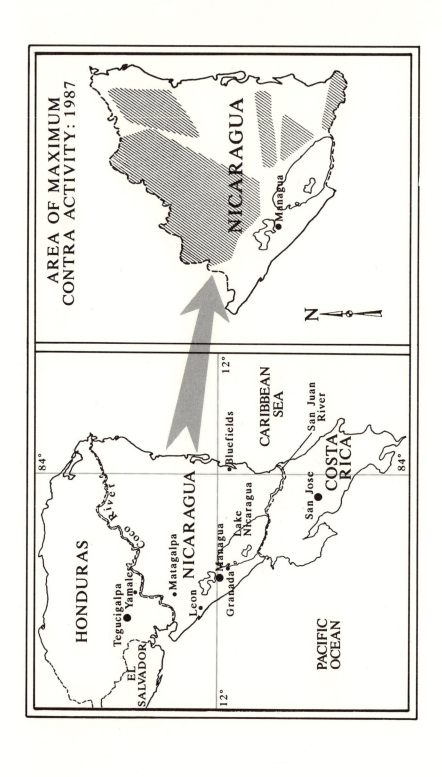

1

Introduction: The Early Years, 1980–1985

Seldom does an individual, let alone a party, emerge from a war in the same shape as it entered. To be sure, there is a principle of continuity. Undying aims are engraved on the soldier's heart as he marches into combat. Untouchable points emblazon the politicians' memoranda as they converge on the baize table. The people's hope turns always toward peace. But men pass and die, and so do ideas. New ones replace the old, driving the wheel. War has no place for anything static.

It is false to think of the contenders in Nicaragua's long civil war as frozen monoliths or to conceive of their antagonism in static terms. Yet how frequently people do that, particularly in the United States. Perhaps the truth of the saying that the generals are always fighting the previous war derives from the fact that the politicians compel them to do so. In a highly dynamic situation, sometimes it seems as if debate has not progressed beyond the arguments of 20 years ago. This results from ignorance and fear; the Vietnam War made Americans wary of the world and mistrustful of themselves.

Fear, insofar as it breeds prudence, is no defect. Ignorance, however, deserves no apology. Reams have been written on tiny Nicaragua, but not enough has been based on knowledge, or even fact. This work is an effort to give a brief account of the rebels.

One hears so much about American involvement in Nicaragua that it is almost impossible to conceive that the counterrevolution had causes or effects remote from the United States. Yet armed resistance to the Sandinista National Liberation Front (Frente Sandinista de Liberación Nacional or FSLN) began within a year of the triumph, in 1979, of the revolution against President Anastasio Somoza. The rebellion was touched off by "Dimas," a veteran Sandinista hero, in early 1980, at a time when the Carter administration was still providing aid to the Sandinista regime.[1]

Dimas protested the incipient totalitarianism of the regime. He was followed by many others with many motives. Some of these men banded together under such fanciful noms de guerre as the "Sagittarians" and the "Chilotes" (Green Corn), which largely reflected a camaraderie of disaffection. Others suggest a more political purpose—such as the Nicaraguan Democratic Union (Union Democrática Nicaragüense or UDN), the 15th of September Legion, and MILPAS (Milicias Populares Anti-Sandinistas). The MILPAS were composed of ex-Sandinistas.[2] The UDN was joined by veterans of the struggle against Somoza not affiliated with the FSLN. The 15th of September Legion was the rallying point of former National Guard soldiers led by Col. Enrique Bermudez Varela. The contras were thus from the start a composite body.

The most skillful of these groups raised money from Cuban and Nicaraguan exiles and in 1981 received training under the auspices of the Argentine military junta. Toward the end of 1981, some of them merged into the Nicaraguan Democratic Force (Fuerza Democrática Nicaragüense or FDN), under the leadership of Bermudez.

Others conspicuously abstained; many felt it was a historic mistake to have ties of any sort with the old regime. Ironically, the rebel with the highest reputation as a nationalistic leader, Eden Pastora Gomez, was the one most completely subsidized by the U.S. Central Intelligence Agency (CIA).[3] Pastora joined the revolt in early 1982, just as the United States was taking a direct interest in the struggle. During these early years, the superpowers lurked in the shadows, keeping a cautious distance.[4]

The war began as a purely Latin American contest, with the Cubans, Mexicans, and Panamanians abetting the FSLN and the Argentines, and other Central Americans (including the Costa Ricans) abetting the contras. It was then that the war gained its notoriety as a blind, pitiless antagonism in which basic precepts of humanity met with the most uncivil scorn. Much of the propaganda arsenal that exploded in later years was amassed in this early period: images of such trigger-happy ex-National Guard renegades as the murderous "Suicida" and of a Bible-burning Sandinista gestapo, which cut the throat and ears of the evangelical preacher Prudencio Baltodano and left him for dead.

But positive, even romantic, images also arose of courageous, God-fearing freedom fighters and defiant nationalists seeking justice. These symbols were based on powerful, albeit incomplete realities and will linger in Central America's political folklore.

Fables of Latin-American solidarity aside, it must be said that the Argentines had no serious strategic interests in Nicaragua, nor any deep insight into Central American society. They were not prepared—either politically or militarily—for the scale of the uprising they soon had on their hands. By supporting the contras, they had hoped merely to curry favor with the Reagan administration, hoping for a response in kind. When the United States took Great Britain's side in the 1982 Falklands War and President Leopoldo Galtieri's regime began to totter, Argentine involvement faded.

By the time the United States engaged directly with the contras, in 1982–1983, sporadic rebellion had become outright civil war, driven not by mere resentment or lust for revenge, but by rich, historical attitudes. Many people tended to view this war exclusively in terms of its contemporary ideological component, or, even more simply, through the perspective of the East-West struggle; they overlooked much of the purely human character of the struggle. More than any other type of strife in the Western experience, the war in Nicaragua resembled a War of Religion, with its messy tangle of alliances between property, personality, and principle, to say nothing of the trappings of corruption, rancor, and hypocrisy.

The revolt gained momentum as the quality of its objectives improved and as the Sandinistas' social compact—outlined in the Revolutionary Charter of 1979—decayed. The Sandinista government still enjoyed firm support in the major cities of the Pacific zone, particularly Granada and Managua. But thousands of rebels meeting with popular acclaim operated in the north, led by Bermudez, and in the south, by the great hero of the revolution, Eden Pastora Gomez. The Indian tribes and the blacks of the Atlantic province were in full revolt against a regime that systematically sought to uproot their unique culture.

Because of proximity, interest, history, and culture, the United States was far better equipped than Argentina to understand Nicaragua. But the United States approached Latin America in general, and Nicaragua in particular, with a lack of gravity that was guaranteed to breed mischief and ill will.

The policy of the United States was not straightforward. Under President Jimmy Carter it supported the Sandinistas. Then it dropped them. Under President Ronald Reagan, it ignored them. Then it supported the contras, secretly. Then it said it did not. Then it supported them openly, but said this was to stop the flow of arms to Communist guerrillas in El Salvador. This came as news to the contras, who could care less about El Salvador. Then the United States dropped the contras. Such an approach made for vast gulfs between rhetoric and reality.

The early execution of U.S. policy was as flawed as its rationale. A covert program may well be suitable to abet a conspiracy, a minuscule revolt, or even an enormous but mysterious insurrection, thousands of miles removed from scrutiny—as in Afghanistan or Angola. But to some Americans, Managua was closer than Washington, D.C. U.S. citizens, many of them deeply committed to the Sandinista regime, traveled daily to Managua and lived the consequences of war. The questions of what to do and how to do it were bound to be contentious in the minds of a political generation that came of age during the Vietnam War.

The CIA was asked to carry out tasks for which it was the wrong instrument, and it became damaged in the process. Its shortcomings, however, were obscured by the early blunders of the Sandinistas and by the contras' successes at recruitment and in military operations. Confidence in the genuine strengths of the cause was displaced by a vulgar bravado. By 1983, many contras and supporters affirmed that "the end of the war was in sight."[5] But the frailty of the Reagan administration's approach was exposed in 1984, when news about the mining of Nicaraguan harbors by the CIA touched off an international scandal and led Congress to reject the policy.

This account begins at that point. Five years after the revolt began, the wildly varying aims of the Sandinistas' foes began to coalesce, and the purpose of the United States in supporting them was clarified at last. In 1985, with the U.S. endorsement of the United Nicaraguan Opposition (Unidad Nicaragüense Opositora or UNO), the Nicaragua policy of the United States at last received a definitive statement. The concept of an "ideal" resistance took shape, a plausible policy and a policy instrument that could lead to worthy ends: the return of peace and the establishment of democratic freedoms in Nicaragua.

How good an instrument of this policy were the contras? By what standard does one proclaim victory or defeat? This account will provide no answer to that question unless the reader brings to bear his own judgment. The writer can only resort to the technique of comparing words and deeds, the "ideal" and the "real" resistance. One must measure such things as the leaders' pledges to freedom against the degree of openness they tolerated in their movement, and their ability to live by the rules they set for themselves against the appeals for justice and due process; one must also evaluate their efforts to resolve the contradictions between the urges of a voluntary army and the discipline required in a republican democracy.

The score will be mixed. With some, the contradictions will be trivial and indicative only of how even the best must compromise with an imperfect world. With others, the discrepancy will be great and suggestive of shameful and dishonorable shortcomings. In yet other cases it will prove fruitless to distinguish between the true and the false purposes. Bernard Mandeville's observation on the English Civil War is a useful reminder of human nature:

> Many of those, who should be too wicked to be Hypocrites, and to counterfeit long, would sometimes not only pray in Good Earnest, but likewise, sent on by the Example before them, be transported with real Zeal for the Good of the Cause.[6]

This is, then, a history of how the rebels came to embrace a certain set of objectives in 1985, their tortuous effort throughout 1986 to establish an institution that could achieve those objectives, the collapse of that initiative and a renewed effort in 1987, and the setbacks that overturned that second effort in 1988.

Readers expecting an expose of lurid crimes will be disappointed, as will those expecting a panegyric. Such tracts are built on myths, noble images, and heroic ideals. Reality is more complicated, for it must encompass not only those things, but others—by far more strange, contradictory, absurd, and human.

2

1985: The Ideal Resistance

§§   How the Reagan administration was chastened by
the Congress in 1984, leading to a change in its
Nicaraguan policy, and why this made it impossible to
continue U.S. support for the fractious spectrum of
contra groups

Exposure of the CIA's mining of Nicaraguan harbors in
1984 unleashed a powerful tide against the contras. Contradictions between the ends and means of the Reagan administration's policy in Nicaragua led Congress to disown the
rebels. The Reagan administration was exposed to charges
of incoherence and intransigence—the products of a certain
disingenuity in its approach. Congress also demanded a
greater say in the crafting of policy. It cut aid, banned CIA
links with the contras, and intensified pressure on the administration to undertake negotiations with the Sandinista
government—irrespective, it seemed, of the content of such
talks. The contras paid dearly for all this: their columns
were forced to an ignominious retreat across the Coco River
into Honduras, taking with them their dreams of a victory
march through Managua.

Some lessons were nonetheless preserved from the debacle. Karl von Clausewitz, the great nineteenth century mil-

itary theorist, wrote that "war is the continuation of politics by other means." This well-known dictum had served in
the White House as a formula to justify the substitution of
politics by war; in 1984, defeat served to underscore the
continuity between the two. The FSLN's skill had contrast-
ed with the administration's crudeness. Politics had served
the FSLN to reap a military victory.

The U.S. administration insisted that political pressure
alone could not free Nicaragua. But Congress remained
skeptical that the contras could be worked into a coherent
political strategy. The chronic problem was disunity, manifested in a cluster of rebel military commands: FDN,
ARDE, FRS, FARN, KISAN, MISURA, and BOS, not to
mention the inchoate galaxy of political, labor, youth, religious, ethnic, and other civic bodies that embraced the
armed resistance with greater or lesser fervor. Their political views ran the gamut from radical Trotskyism to mysti-
cal Catholicity. The largest faction, the FDN, seemed at
best a blind, ill-disciplined force, with only pro forma civilian control. The contras seemed to devote more energy to
quarrels among themselves than to fighting the Sandinistas. In sum, they were not an attractive alternative, and it
looked as if they could never win.

Between the two positions—of diplomacy or force—
there was a middle ground. To breach it, the administration's thinking realigned toward a combination of diplomatic efforts backed by the indigenous military sanction that
would in due course become its "ideal" resistance. But for
such a two-track policy to regain the confidence of the Congress, two preconditions would have to be fulfilled: talks
with the Sandinistas and unity in the contras.

The administration therefore took one step back in order to take two steps forward. It opened with the FSLN a
bilateral dialogue, known as the Manzanillo forum, after the
Mexican town in which the meetings took place. But the
U.S. administration was chary of implicitly legitimizing the
Sandinista regime and doubted that the FSLN had moder-
ated its revolutionary ambitions since 1982, when it had

rejected a nonaggression pact proposed by Assistant Secretary of State for Inter-American Affairs Thomas Enders. The administration thus wanted to distract hopes away from the Manzanillo forum, though without appearing to be bent on a purely military approach.

A Nicaraguan national dialogue—a gathering of the contras, the Sandinistas, and the internal opposition—that would be suitably reinforced by regional talks between the five Central American republics could serve this purpose. The problem was to make such a process a desirable substitute or precondition for bilateral U.S.-Nicaragua talks. The internal opposition lacked the strength, and the contras were too divided to be taken seriously. The Reagan administration thus set out to persuade the fractious contras to sink their differences into a common democratic front.

§§   How the FDN, the largest contra group, had been pursuing a false strategy because of errors in its view of Nicaraguan society

The errors of the contras have received more superficial attention than those of the U.S. administration, yet their damage went deeper. In this respect a cautionary word is in order. The reader will observe that the shortcomings of the FDN are of primary concern for this paper. This is because the FDN, as the largest faction, had the greatest say on the shape of the war. But all the factions can be faulted for foggy thinking; though sharpened considerably after 1985, the low caliber of their early political pronouncements will persuade the reader of as much.

The errors of the FDN and the Reagan administration are often difficult to distinguish from each other. One can point, for example, to bad intelligence from the United States, which mismeasured the pace of decay of the FSLN's social compact. Pressure to come up with scenarios that would "sell" in Washington had cast the war in an unrealistic time frame. This inflamed the wishful thinking that prevailed in the civilian leadership of the FDN. "Next year in Managua!" was the slogan of 1983 used by the Hondurans and Costa Ricans in 1987 to reproach both the U.S. administration and the contras.[1]

Many in the FDN viewed the Sandinistas simply as a more successful version of the Somozas—not exactly an unwarranted outlook, for the continuity between the old and the new regimes is in many ways more remarkable than the change. But the FDN failed to perceive that a difference in quality had become a difference in kind. Nicaragua under the Sandinistas was really quite a new thing.

The strength of the old regime had derived from the atomization of social forces. By contrast, the strength of the new was in its vision of total mobilization around a centralized, revolutionary purpose. The frailty of civil society under the old regime is what made possible the vigor of the state in the new. The root of the Sandinista order was the classical Leninist paradox of a strong state in a weak society.

From this system radiated a network of dependence and duties, of reward and punishment, and, in short, of what Jean-François Revel describes when he notes that in a totalitarian society "everyone has a vested interest in tension." *Sandinismo* permeated Nicaraguan life, politicizing all things: the parallel church, the schools, unions, hospitals, women's clubs, youth groups. There was no shape it could not assume. The most alarming sign of this ductility was the melding of the Army into the apparatus of Party and State, the three strands upholding the Sandinista power structure.

Over time, such a system might well relax its grip or be oxidized by discontent and boredom. But once consolidated, the oppressive, revolutionary form would remain, unless actively shattered by the society it itself had molded. The collective act of will that such a reaction requires is many orders of magnitude more awesome than the popular outbursts that unseat the old-style dictatorships. One must ask whether the ends justify the means.

Time was not on the side of the contras. They were in a race against the consolidation of the new Sandinista order of society. Furthermore, their U.S. support was too unstable and their own alliance too fragile to augur well for long-term plans.

Yet the FDN leadership, guided by the U.S. administration, once again fought the war of 1979, which had taken the Sandinistas nearly 20 years to win. Even at the height of their success in 1984, the rebels knew that they—like the FSLN against the National Guard—did not have the strength to destroy the government force in a direct clash. Just as the tiny cells of the FSLN had done with Somoza, the FDN planned to win by default. The FDN's scenario had been set for victory in the event that it could escape defeat.

This meant exploding the myths underpinning the regime—above all, its invincibility—to show Nicaraguans that the FDN offered a viable alternative. The army and secret police had to be spread thin. It had to be shown that, contrary to revolutionary propaganda, the FSLN was not everywhere, nor supported by everyone. The corrosion of the regime—manifested in economic chaos, defections, and moral decadence—would combine with popular unrest to touch off outbursts in the cities. A "little push," adequately backed by the United States, was all that would be needed to bring the FSLN power structure crashing down.

Thus it was easy to charge that the contras had no strategy but simply to sit and wait till the winds of change shook the Sandinistas from the trees. Many in the FDN leadership regarded their own efforts as diversionary, intended to mark time until U.S. Marines landed to do the shaking. After Grenada, many Nicaraguans on both sides of the struggle were easily persuaded that the invasion was but a matter of time. The relaxed commands of Bermudez did not help. As one combatant complained, "[Bermudez] would simply point to Nicaragua and say, 'Go see what you can do there. And good luck.'"

There were sound reasons to steer clear of the cities.

The FDN's rural-based plan was in many respects like Tomás Borge's strategy of Prolonged Popular War (Guerra
Popular Prolongada or GPP). The social base of the resistance was rooted in the *campesinos*, especially in the prov-
inces of Jinotega and Chontales. Equally important, the
cities were off-limits to the rebels. There, a crucial organizational advantage held for the FSLN, which bolstered its
urban-based program with first-class tools for surveillance
and social control. It is not without irony that these tools
were now managed by Borge himself, as minister of
interior.

But if this cautious strategy made military sense, it
cost the contras in political credibility. Urban insurrection
had been relegated to a passive role in the struggle, and
long into 1986, links between the contras and the internal
opposition remained exploratory. For the FDN, political ac-
tivism suggested little more than the steady emission of
press releases and the keeping of a certain area of wall
sprayed with fresh subversive slogans to encourage the pop-
ulace. Insurrections would more or less "happen" when the
"beginning of the end" had arrived.

Even with such a crude political base the FDN had had
remarkable success. But under the surface, powerful tides
were ripping at its gains. The brusque manner in which the
United States dropped the rebels in 1984 to some extent
obscured those tides and breathed life into a myth: if only
Congress had not flip-flopped, the FDN would now be in
Managua. This bred the attitude that an ideologically inclu-
sive political approach was but a necessary evil: a sop to
Congress, not a good in itself.

In hindsight, it is evident that such an approach would
fail. Support for the FSLN had clearly ebbed, and everywhere there were hopeful signs for the contras—riots in the
popular quarter of Monimbó, spontaneous risings against
the draft in Matagalpa and Jinotega, and a pervasive disillusionment asserted in countless small acts of personal resistance. But Daniel Ortega could still draw a high-spirited
throng to the Plaza of Heroes and Martyrs, as shown by the

festivities for his inauguration as president in February 1985. The FSLN's power structure was far less brittle than had been supposed and would certainly not collapse of its own weight.

§§ Why so many Nicaraguans who opposed the Sandinistas, even with armed force, were reluctant to tie their fortunes to the FDN

Many Nicaraguans who opposed the FSLN had foreseen these problems. Such figures as Arturo Cruz,[2] "El Negro" Chamorro,[3] Alfredo Cesar Aguirre,[4] Alfonso Robelo,[5] and Eden Pastora led the struggle to reform and broaden the contras and admired President Reagan's commitment to their cause. They also saw that without U.S. support, they could not succeed against the Soviet-backed FSLN.[6] Nevertheless these leaders had remained aloof from the FDN, the main instrument of the administration's policy, believing that the fight would fail unless it wheeled around both political and military criteria. They talked of strength as well as legitimacy, arguing that a redesigned policy would induce Nicaragua's internal opposition groups to join a broad revolutionary front like that of 1979.

Indeed, their common interest was to recapture the revolution. Most had actively struggled against Somoza; many had been Sandinistas, some of high rank. Among them were many ex-Trotskyites whose faith undertook a democratic leap when confronted by the ugliness of raw power. They hated not only the FSLN's tyranny, but its betrayal of Nicaragua's democratic destiny.

Some of these figures occupied a self-conscious position between the armed resistance and the internal opposition, and they sought to narrow the gap separating the two. Chief among them was Arturo Cruz, a former Sandinista ambassador to Washington. In 1984 he stood for the presidency as the candidate for an alliance of democratic parties in the internal opposition known as the Nicaraguan Democratic Coordinator. In late 1984, still bristling over the way the Interior Ministry gangs had roughed him up during the campaign from which he had withdrawn, Cruz expressed an interest in joining the armed struggle. In January 1985, along with Pedro Joaquin Chamorro, son of the *La Prensa* editor whose assassination in 1978 had touched off the insurrection against Somoza, Cruz publicly endorsed military aid to the contras.[7]

Some of Cruz's one-time political associates had already turned to armed resistance via Eden Pastora's army in the south. Alfonso Robelo had been a member of the original junta that replaced Somoza; Cesar had been the secretary of the junta, for which he drafted the since-forsaken revolutionary charter (the "Sandinista promises"). Both now joined with Arturo Cruz and Adolfo Calero, the head of the FDN, to negotiate a common front.[8]

These men, with their respective camps, pursued a fascinating range of motives: some noble, some irrational, and some banal. But they were alike in their hard calculation that a U.S. guarantee of their political identity was key to their success in a unified resistance. They mistrusted the FDN, or hoped to extract concessions from it. Only the Reagan administration could resolve the contradiction between their urge to unite—without which their struggle would be in vain—and their fear of being conquered by their own ally. These fears, and the problem of the U.S. guarantee, were the predominant forces shaping the armed resistance.

The background of these men equipped them well to sympathize with the way U.S. moderates reasoned about Nicaragua. They understood the need for "cover" in the Congress, and they saw the possibility of building a coalition among those who asked for it. Arturo Cruz, Jr., an adviser to his father, argued in late 1984 that

> the Reagan administration has to give credit to the Democrats, whose pressure makes reform in the "counterrevolution" possible. The liberals need their own pre-

text, as with El Salvador, to approve the aid themselves. We have to find our own Duarte to lay the base
for a bipartisan consensus. Then the liberals can say
that they do not necessarily approve of the policies of
the Reagan administration, but rather are approving
aid in order to strengthen the center, and Nicaraguan
democrats.[9]

Most U.S. Democrats adamantly opposed the contras. But
some did not do so on principle; they simply deplored the
practice of the administration. When Cruz—the unimpeach-
able democrat—began to talk of joining the rebel movement, there was strong interest from these congressmen,
whose numbers sufficed to tilt the balance on the issue.
Subsequent legislative battles over Nicaragua were fought
over this narrow turf of about 30 Democratic Congressmen,
the so-called swing voters.

§§ Why the new vision of the struggle concentrated on the politics of insurrection

Nineteen eighty-five was the year in which politics became important to the contras. The new contras tilted the
movement's thinking toward a new concept of struggle that
made it possible to see things in more realistic proportions:
Nicaragua's tortuous history, its dealings with the Congress, its problem of symmetry with El Salvador, and the
dynamics of superpower rivalry.

The new concept envisioned a more active undermining
of the Sandinista power structure. It recognized that the
resistance would have to undergo reform and political
growth before it could offer a serious alternative to the Sandinistas. The challenge for the administration, the new contras, and the FDN would be how to manage this growth,
how to balance (in the Nicaraguans' own terms) "quotas of
power" consistent with not only the historical reality of the
contra movement but the concerns of Nicaraguan society as
a whole.

The views of the new contras centered on theories of insurrection and converged with the administration's gropings toward a so-called two-track policy. To be sure, the notion of urban uprisings—complete with barricades in the popular quarters and marches of workers, students, and little old ladies—was a feature of all discussions on how to overthrow the Sandinistas. But its place in an overall strategy was not very well thought out.

The internal opposition—and the political space within Nicaragua—thus became an object of the new contras' careful attention. Hitherto each group had regarded the other more as a competitor than a partner in one continuous spectrum of opposition. In this more comprehensive strategy, the military push of a united resistance would go hand in hand with the repudiation of the regime by a broad internal front. The continuum between war and politics would be affirmed.

Among the internal opposition, there prevailed an uneasy awareness of the connection between the narrow political space available to them and the fortunes of the resistance. As Enrique Bolaños, the leader of the private enterprise sector in the internal opposition, explained, "They are Public Enemy #1, and we are Public Enemy #2; when they are gone, we will be Public Enemy #1."[10]

Many in the internal opposition courageously repudiated the regime and publicly refused to condemn aid to the contras, sometimes at great personal risk. Yet the bulk of them simply could not call for an uprising that seemed so likely to flush out the FSLN in favor of mere anarchy or yet another armed corps checked only by its own word as happened in 1979. Some felt a duty to serve as loyal opposition to the FSLN. Some in principle opposed military force. The charge that the absence of firm U.S. support prevented them from throwing their lot in with the contras is only partly true. The precept for this group was "once bitten, twice shy." Until 1987, for reasons ranging from well-grounded qualms to the shameless careerism of the *zanganos* (drones living off the toil of others) and *zancudis-*

tas (mosquitoes living off others' blood), the internal opposition remained divided on whether to reject the FSLN or to work within the system to modify it into "something like the Mexican PRI."

Democratic intent was not enough. If the gap between armed resistance and internal opposition were to close, change would be necessary for the contras, not only in their way of thinking, but in their way of acting. The unbridled dreams of Pastora and the narrow leadership of the FDN alarmed many. Proof was needed of deep-rooted democratic structures. The resistance would have to woo and protect the internal opposition rather than compete with it.

§§   How the new contras began to exert an influence on the congressional balance of power as certain Democrats perceived a shift in the Reagan administration's policy

What did all of these developments signify? That there was a convergence of interests between the first raft of disillusioned revolutionaries, the Reagan administration, and the FDN. In March, Adolfo Calero, Arturo Cruz, and Alfonso Robelo outlined the convergence in the Declaration of San Jose, a proposal for a church-mediated dialogue that was at once endorsed by President Reagan.

The moderate Democrats received the declaration with great interest. Many of them supported the president's policy in El Salvador, but opposed it in Nicaragua because of the lack of symmetry in his approach to the two countries. At this point, a notable restatement of the administration's policy seemed to be taking place. Bruce Cameron, an influential liberal Democratic lobbyist, observed that

> in 1984 the Administration would not even mention the idea of dialogue between the Nicaraguan government and its opposition. To do so would give credence to dialogue in El Salvador, which it then opposed.

Enter Napoleon Duarte, who made dialogue ac-
ceptable overnight when he invited Salvadoran rebels
to meet him at La Palma, El Salvador, in October, 1984.
Next Arturo Cruz godfathered the San Jose proposal of
March 1, 1985. That declaration does not call for an
overthrow, but for a national dialogue leading to new
Assembly elections. In that proposal, President Ortega
could only be removed as a result of a plebiscite.

The human rights/dialogue formula was working in
El Salvador. The Administration seemed to be moving
towards a similar formula in Nicaragua.[11]

Were that indeed the case, Cameron and most of the swing
voters felt the president should be supported. They began
to work with the administration to craft a legislative package that would do this.

After the Sandinistas rejected the dialogue proposal, as
expected, the president requested $14 million in military
aid for the contras. It would be some time, however, before
the two-track concept would pay off. The Declaration of San
Jose reflected primarily an informal convergence of principles; it was not enough to satisfy the U.S. Congress that the
administration had changed the substance, rather than just
the style, of its policy. President Reagan's request failed on
April 24, as the House voted nay, 180–245.

The cutoff did not modify the Sandinistas' behavior.
Stories of abuse of government and Marxist bravado continued to flow from Managua. Relations between Nicaragua
and the United States failed to sweeten even a little as, a
few days after the House vote, President Ortega traveled to
Moscow. The case may not have been clear for those who
said that the contras put positive pressure on the Sandinistas. But Ortega's flight made those look ridiculous who had
said that disowning the contras would help mollify the Sandinistas. The FSLN seemed poised to take an even harder
line.

The swing voters continued to be available for a bipartisan coalition. But first they demanded substantive changes
in the administration's approach to show that it would fol-

low a genuine two-track policy. From the rebels they demanded unity, reform, and negotiations.

The administration took up this offer. The April 24 vote for $14 million was its last try for military aid with an unreconstructed FDN. Its own allies recognized that a two-track approach was essential and that it would not work without change in the contras. The administration thus intensified its pressure on the rebels to form a broad front and tried to make common ground with the swings.

§§   **Personal more than political differences were the great hindrance to the reorganization of the contras—and the most notorious distraction from unity**

Much has been made of the contras' personal and political differences. Truly, when it comes to Nicaraguan affairs, whoever tries to draw a distinction between them will obtain nothing but a headache. The rebel leaders all marched under different political symbols, which assuredly would have meant much were they ever to hold the reins of power. But the political contrasts among the contras, however sharp, over time tended to fade. The contras, more often at the mercy of events than actively shaping them, usually had few choices. Yet the individuals who struggled to take charge over them were never fewer. The most aggravating obstacles to unity were, more often than not, *people* rather than *policies*.

By personal differences one should not imagine simply whimsical, petulant, or childish conceits. With such feuds the resistance was rife, as is any political assembly; but by and large the contras were ready to swallow their pride for the sake of temporary personal advantage or even the common good. Far more important was the fact that personal differences translated into differences in administrative style and staffs. The struggle for position accounted for much of the sordid picture of contra infighting. The "lists" parceling out the posts of the resistance—some of which were virtual sinecures—became the ground over which wrestled the outs and the ins. The precarious institutions of the resistance were too feeble to channel its members' ambitions to a good end.

The tangled relations between people, power, and policy are typified by the inability of the administration to persuade Pastora and Cesar to join UNO. Both men were recognized as assets of great potential. But there was considerable reluctance to meet their demands more than halfway. The enthusiasm that they aroused on one account, they dissipated on the other. Political outlook had something to do with this perception, but the main issue was reliability. Pastora had charisma, but was disorganized and unstable; Cesar was adroit, but was notorious as a double-crosser.

A venerable hero of the revolution, Pastora was the ideal contra figurehead, if only he would have been happy with that. Unfortunately he was like the king who wanted not only to grace the stamps, but to run the post office too. He delegated everything, then insisted on doing things himself. Notoriously, he undercut his own aides. "He always wanted to be the great *cazique* [chief], and because of his suspicions made it impossible to do anything," complained one of his combatants in Costa Rica, shortly after passing over to the FDN.[12] Indeed, by 1985, the five commanders of the Alianza Revolucionaria Democrática (ARDE), exasperated by Pastora's messianic attitudes, were under his authority on paper only. "Every so often he would go roll around in the mud and then give a press conference, but we did our own thing."[13] The troops loyal to Pastora by this time numbered only about 150. By presiding over the alliance, Pastora brought it international legitimacy but little else.

By contrast, no one was comfortable with the thought of Cesar in a position of high visibility. He had an uncanny ability to erect a public image, but had no popular following, which made him something of a loose wheel. His influence derived largely from convenient alliances, in which he straddled the balance of power. His reputation as the one who would be first to cut a deal with the Sandinistas was to become a valuable asset in 1987, when bona fide negotiations were the fashion. In 1985, however, when the rebels still hoped for a military victory, it was a handicap. Even Cruz mistrusted him and was hardly on speaking terms with his former partner on "Rescate de la Revolucion," who behind his back had traveled to Managua for talks with the FSLN in 1984.

Cesar had hoped to use his Social-Democratic splinter group, Bloque Opositor del Sur (BOS), to garner a seat on the directorate of the new organization, which would need an odd number of members to prevent stalemate between Cruz and Calero. But Calero balked at the notion of treating Cesar, 34-year-old head of a microscopic faction, as an equal. Cruz could not stand him, and supporters in the United States thought him unsound. Robelo was the logical choice for the third seat. He was also young, although by then internationally respected as a former member of the Sandinista provisional junta, president of the Democratic Coordinator, and a leader of strikes against Somoza.

Cruz's followers did not disregard Cesar's political and administrative acumen. Sensing a general identity of purpose, they tried from Costa Rica to enlist him as an ally, in a position analogous to what later became the General Secretariat of UNO. This potentially vital office would have put in his hands not only the directorate's agenda, but also the burgeoning bureaucracy of the resistance. Cesar would have been, in the words of one Cruz follower, "not a senior, but the senior of the juniors. In time, he could become one of the seniors. But he wouldn't take that. He had to be on the front pages of the *New York Times*, or he wouldn't play at all."[14]

Cesar's gifts could only satisfy him from a commanding height; Pastora's objectives were vague but incompatible with obscurity or small influence. Well has it been said that every would-be statesman believes it his first duty to get power and his second duty to keep it. Cesar and Pastora wanted both the symbols and the substance of power. Nobody would yield these to them.

§§   How UNO was at last chartered, stressing unity and promising reform and negotiations

At the last minute Cesar and Pastora stepped aside. So did some of the Miskito Indian groups and other secondary figures. But the Reagan administration's first pick—Robelo, Cruz, and the Indian force KISAN—were available. On June 12, the same day that the administration reached a compromise with the swing voters, they joined with the FDN under the umbrella UNO.[15] UNO's birthday present was a $27 million package of humanitarian aid.

Different motives drove these deals. The "swings" wanted negotiations, to avoid the nasty choice of all-out war or surrender. The administration wanted a congressional majority, to regain control over the policy. The new contras wanted reform, to forge a broad front. The FDN wanted aid, so it could keep fighting.

UNO was thus born out of a temporary convergence of motives, some of which contradicted one another. But to have institutionalized the convergence was a vital qualitative leap. Without a vehicle for unity, there could be no hope for the contras. UNO gave institutional life to the ideal statement of the two-track policy toward which the United States had inched since 1983, when it imposed a civilian directorate on the FDN as a condition for further aid. The reader will find that much of the contras' story hereafter turns around the effort to reconcile the ideal and the real resistance.

The new contras anticipated a schedule of administrative and political reform and had cried that "the civilians should control the military, and the civilian wing should be politically balanced." They took UNO at face value and stressed unity, diversity, and equilibrium. But from the start UNO's composition signified that there was to be trade-off between these three.

For reasons of bureaucratic inertia alone, this would be true. Robelo recalls: "I represented a civilian, political organization. The FDN was an army, with its own objectives and its own way of acting. That gave it, in practice, much more weight than all of our civic organizations combined."[16]

In fact, a host of contradictions would bedevil the reformers' efforts. Attention focused from the start on the tense relations between Cruz and Calero, the director of the FDN. They made light of their differences, stressing their common purpose. But neither took pains to hide that the political equilibrium of UNO was unnatural, obeying neither the organizational needs of the movement as a whole, nor its history. Cruz, who realized he would be the outsider in a game of insiders and outsiders, hoped to overcome this disadvantage by

- earning the trust of the combatants, with his reputation as a national, democratic figure;
- encouraging those who had supported him as the Democratic Coordinator's candidate to close ranks with the armed resistance;
- using the support from the Reagan administration; and
- serving as the key to a bipartisan consensus in the U.S. Congress.

The reformers aimed to put the new balance on a more natural footing by attracting new recruits and weeding out some of the old ones—particularly ex-National Guardsmen in the military hierarchy. Their ultimate objective was to institutionalize the democratic character of the resistance. Cruz recognized that he could not do this alone. "We depended on a sort of American guarantee," said Robelo, in order to preserve, let alone manage, the balance.

§§   What the FDN was, why it had such weight in
UNO, and why it was hostile to the new contras

Whether composed of holdouts from the old regime,
dissidents from the new, or simply civilians, the FDN had
been the most successful of many armed bands that had
risen against the FSLN. Under the leadership of Col. Enrique Bermudez,[17] who founded the original nucleus of FDN,
and of Adolfo Calero, who had been imposed on the corps as
a condition of U.S. aid early in 1983, the FDN had crafted a
simple political message with strong appeal. It recruited
from all walks of life in Nicaragua. By 1984, it managed the
largest *campesino* insurrection in Latin America since the
Mexican revolution of 1910. The FDN had about as many
combatants as the Salvadoran guerrillas at their peak in
1981 and nearly four times what the FSLN had fielded in
1979.

Key elements of the FDN's success were its respect for
traditional values of family and the free community, in particular a commitment to upholding religious freedoms, a
most important right in such a God-fearing country. The
FDN's strength was that it adhered to no particular political doctrine; its followers were motivated mostly by a spirit
of individualism, enterprise, and *el derecho de vivir tran-
quilo* (the right to mind one's own business).

Without contradicting what has been said above, one
could point also to bully tactics, sloganeering, scant regard
for public opinion, meanness, petty corruption, a vengeful
spirit, and abject dependence on the United States. The
FDN's shortcomings, particularly in its early years, are obvious. Despite them—indeed, some might argue because of
them—it was the body that best answered to the thousands
of Nicaraguans who offered life and limb in the fight
against the FSLN. One always had a choice, but most of
those who wanted to fight went to the FDN.

It is false to argue that the FDN was not an authenti-
cally Nicaraguan movement. The problem with FDN was
precisely its authenticity. The FDN was an accurate reflec-

tion of Nicaraguan society, no less and no more than the Sandinista Front. Indeed, the problem with both movements was that they seemed to incarnate rather than transcend Nicaragua's ghoulish history. Their appeal to the nation as a whole thus fell short.

Why did the FDN prove so resistant to change? The answer is not hard to find. It had traditions and institutional pride; it was tightly run; it was a *fait accompli*. Many of its men regarded the passage to UNO not as a natural development but as an imposition, warranted only by the compromise that it would bring further U.S. supplies. "Calero even bargained away our name, FDN, which we the combatants had chosen ourselves," complained a foot soldier. Many in the rank and file were particularly galled at pledging allegiance to Cruz and Robelo, who once had represented the Sandinistas in Washington or sat with them on the junta in Managua. They had strong misgivings that the politicians would skip the movement as easily as they had joined, to make their own peace with the Sandinistas.

The FDN leadership did little to mitigate these feelings. If anything, it inflamed them with assurances that nothing would change in the new alliance, in which the FDN's institutional identity was preserved as "UNO-FDN." Its confidence is best symbolized in the redesigned logo, in which a dark-blue FDN is brazenly imposed on the pale and barely legible outline of UNO.

As mentioned, political differences between the old contras and the new proved largely susceptible to a painless resolution. An organizational problem is what thwarted Cruz and Robelo. The FDN was an army, with a bureaucracy attached. It was geared to military and administrative, not political, activity. Only as the challenge of resisting the Sandinistas became more complex and as international diplomatic intervention made even more arcane the problem of dealing with the U.S. Congress would the FDN itself realize that it simply was not equipped to fight the Sandinistas alone. Pressure emerged from its own ranks to adapt to the changing circumstances.

§§   How the contradictory motives of UNO's sponsors
in the Reagan administration and in Congress
undermined the effort to reform the movement

For Congress, other things were more important in mid-
1985 than reform in the contras. The year had been dominated by the failure of the Manzanillo talks, continued stag-
nation in Contadora, and Ortega's flight to Moscow. The
desire to chasten Ortega was strong, yet the poor showing
in April of the $14 million military aid vote showed that
Congress was not ready to embrace an unadorned military
track. Talks with Nicaragua were its main concern.

Most congressmen judged contra reform simply as a
political feat to be measured in terms of a willingness to
negotiate. They were chary of the president's open-ended
commitment and did not want to underwrite an intransi-
gent position. In this respect, reality fell short of the administration's hopes that the association of Cruz's moderating
influence with Calero would reassure the swing voters.

The "swings" wanted a specific avowal from the president that his policy was guided by political and not military
aims. Unlike their liberal colleagues, the "swings" were not
bent on forcing the administration into direct talks with
Managua. Rep. Dave McCurdy (D-Okla.), for instance,
seems to have required only that the president forswear a
military overthrow of the FSLN. But of the contras as a
precondition for U.S. support, he insisted on a willingness
to engage in a political process with the regime.

These guarantees were obtained by—of all people—Lt.
Col. Oliver North, in the form of a widely noted letter from
the president:

> Our policy for Nicaragua is the same as for El Salvador
> and all of Central America: to support the democratic
> center against the extremes of both the right and left,
> and to secure democracy and lasting peace through na-
> tional dialogue and regional negotiations. We do not
> seek the military overthrow of the Sandinista govern-

ment, or to put in its place a government based on supporters of the old Somoza regime . . . executive authority in Nicaragua should change only through elections.[18]

The president also spelled out his position on bilateral talks between the United States and Nicaragua, noting that he would instruct a special ambassador to consult with regional leaders and UNO

> as to how and when the U.S. could resume useful direct talks with Nicaragua. However, such talks cannot be a substitute for a church-mediated dialogue between the contending factions and the achievement of a workable Contadora agreement. Therefore I will have our representatives meet again with representatives of Nicaragua only when I determine that such a meeting would be helpful in promoting these ends.[19]

On June 12, the same day as UNO's chartering, the U.S. House voted 248–184 to provide $27 million in humanitarian aid to the contras. This aid included food, medical supplies, and certain transportation services.

The House majority was comfortable, but rested on shaky ground, for the June vote was not so much a show of confidence in the contras as it was a censure of the Sandinistas. There had been no time to judge the results of reform; unlike the burning topic of negotiations, Congress hardly considered this issue at all. Bruce Cameron warned that because of this, the swing Democrats were making "a lot of risky bets"

1. that the president's letter is believable;
2. that the main contra force, the FDN, can be reformed and will settle for less than overthrowing the Sandinistas;
3. that the Salvadoran government will negotiate in good faith; and
4. that either the Sandinistas or the Salvadoran guer-

rillas are prepared to make a historic compromise
through negotiations. . . .[20]

Cameron added: "Whether Cruz and Robelo, who have both
[sic] acknowledged the FDN's human rights abuses in the
past, and who want a political solution, will be able to share
real authority with Calero and the FDN military leadership
is still up in the air."[21]

§§ How the humanitarian aid compromise confused matters and soon allowed both Congress and the White House to shirk their commitments to upholding a two-track policy

In practice, the humanitarian aid compromise failed to
build broad, bipartisan support for the two-track approach.
Instead, it allowed congressional moderates to take a stance
without having to pay a political price. Thus was set a
pattern that would be repeated in 1987 and 1988. For lack
of a consensus on a decisive course, Congress produced ambiguous legislation and surrendered the initiative. In 1985
the White House was ready and eager to give itself the
broadest possible reading of the Boland Amendment, which
restricted the support U.S. government agencies could provide the contras; in 1987 it would be the Sandinistas' turn
to stretch beyond credulity the text of the Arias peace
plan.
    Neither the Left nor the Right was happy with polite
fictions, and both argued that such a compromise pointed
to moral cowardice. On the Left, Rep. Edward Boland (D-
Mass.) pointed out that the $27 million was more than what
the United States had spent "when we supplied all the contras' needs, military or otherwise." He argued forcefully:
"We are continuing to fund the Contras. They continue to
conduct military operations. Our assistance furthers and
supports those operations."[22] That the contras' military
needs were being met by mysterious sources was indeed an

open secret; Congress had even allowed the CIA greater latitude in training and sharing intelligence with the contras. It was also plain, however, that the United States denied the contras the political support they needed to win such a struggle. The conservatives viewed humanitarian aid as a hypocritical sellout. As former U.S. ambassador to Costa Rica Curtin Winsor observed, "Americans have no business encouraging people to die in vain. To ask for the sacrifice of democratic people for less than democratic victory is immoral."[23]

The humanitarian aid compromise had helped satisfy the physical needs of the contras. It allowed them to survive—even to pick up the fight a bit. But its effect on their political fortunes was indeed mixed. Congress had acted in a manner to suggest it was not taking, but rather testing, a position. The debate was thus entrenched over the movement of positions, not over the positions themselves—matters more of perception than fact. For this reason, much of the political battle in Washington was fought over images and rhetoric and was so sensitive to damning symbolic details.

A sense of proportion was lost. In March 1985, the president's comparison of the contras to the founding fathers invited opponents to a field day in making sport of his contradictions between rhetoric and reality. The Left, by the same token, took liberty to proclaim the new dawn from any dull flicker of moderation from Managua and to clamor for a nonaggression pact between Nicaragua and the United States.

The only ones who could lose in such a contest were the reformers. The chartering of UNO had not constituted change—but a promise of change—in return for aid. The FDN and the Reagan administration had obtained, up front, what they wanted. Calero had merely to string out superficial concessions to keep the Cruz people expectant and to cover the moderates from one vote to the next. The intemperate charges even of many centrist contra opponents meant that the administration could hold its ground in Congress by a judicious management of the rebels' reputation as monsters.

Like the FDN, the administration saw reform not as desirable in itself but chiefly as a tool to pry out aid. The swing voters, on the other hand, dared not be seen advocating the use of military force. Nor would they allow the contras to play a policy role as anything other than a political entity. The twin components of the two-track policy were thus estranged at birth.

§§   Cruz

Where did this leave the reformers? They were pretty much alone in their quest for change. A suspicion lingers among the followers of Cruz that the Reagan administration betrayed him. Bent as it was on a militaristic adventure, it failed to support him—if it did not deliberately undermine him at every turn—against the nefast cabals masterminded by Calero. To this, the Calero camp responds that Cruz always received what he asked for, yet he was never satisfied; he failed due to moral arrogance and his own political ineptitude. To arrive at a proper judgment, one must see what Cruz sought to achieve and how he went about it. As much as one may deplore the school of psychohistorical writing, to understand the contras one must consider the tormented soul of Arturo Cruz.

One could hardly ask for a more poignant instance of Bernard Mandeville's paradox than Arturo Cruz, whose private virtues brought about his ruin as a public figure. Even in his name, he acquired the quality of an easy metaphor in which the agony of the Nicaraguan center was described in puns on the Via Crucis, crusades, crucifixion, and so forth.

His chief political commodity was a universal reputation for decency, which made him a sort of coveted portable shrine, bestowing legitimacy to whatever it was attached—whether the contras, the internal opposition, or, before them, the Sandinista Front.[24] Cruz held the Christian political view that society is a thing created by the mind of men and could after all be improved by men. This translated into an intellectual habit of believing that consensus *must* be attainable and men *would* compromise, if only reason were touched.

Such a trait by no means guaranteed him a rough ride through the political jungle of Nicaragua. After all, blackmail and extortion make as strong an appeal to reason as does the Socratic method. But Cruz shied from such dark instruments. He shared, with none other than Tomás Borge, a belief in the fundamental identity between ends and means. The same view led to different attitudes. Borge built a career based on precepts of rigidity. Cruz found stature because of the paradox that he always compromised. As happens to many a high-principled and well-meaning man, compromise turned his public career into a labyrinth of dilemmas, with ends and means and ends reflecting one another like a warped tunnel of mirrors.

Well may one wonder what drives such a man to the political life, for his willingness to settle for half-a-loaf advertised that Cruz was moved by no vision in particular, let alone anything like the intoxicating utopias that the founders of nations live and breathe. His chief spur to action was the hollow ache of knowing that evil triumphs when good men do nothing. By the same token, he felt obliged to steer only for a better course. Cruz understood that Nicaragua was sick to death of "great leaders" and would rally to a modest man who could be trusted to turn over power. Paradoxically for Cruz, in Nicaragua such an act would have been an act of unprecedented greatness.

§§   Why divisions in the executive branch over the question of negotiations strengthened the hand of Calero

In operative terms, UNO was not really one alliance between Cruz, Robelo, and Calero, but rather a pair of alliances between Cruz and the White House and between Calero and the White House. Nor was the pair symmetrical, though this fact would become clear only as the calls for milestone reform flew by. Oliver North was the pivotal figure in each alliance, the charioteer behind the unruly tandem. Elliott Abrams was the herald, proclaiming its rickety career.

Cruz's authority in UNO had the same origin as Calero's: he knew how to deal with the Americans; he could deliver. Like Calero, who went to Notre Dame, he was educated in the United States and spoke a language that Americans understand. But his accent reflected the sophisticated detachment of Georgetown, not the straightforward attitudes of South Bend. Cruz's constituency was among those who drew subtle distinctions about Nicaragua—in Congress, the centrists, and within the administration, the State Department's career bureaucrats. Beyond these quarters, Cruz commanded scant recognition. As one young conservative explained, "Cruz talked negotiations. Calero talked victory. Viet Nam showed us that there can be no substitute for victory."

To be sure, negotiations were at the heart of Cruz's political strategy. He was not naive or overly righteous; unlike many of his counterparts on the congressional Left, Cruz argued as strongly as Calero that the only law the Sandinistas respected was that of the gun. Nor was he deceived by the limits to support for the rebel cause, be it in Nicaragua or the United States. Violent acts belied the contras' democratic words. To many, the contras seemed to have taken to arms as a first, not last, resort. This tactic had to change; arms had to be proven as the only resort.

Cruz was thus willing to give such negotiating devices as the Contadora process (sponsored by four Latin American nations) a try. He had counted on the Reagan administration to support his moves to isolate the FSLN abroad and at home and link with the internal parties as a "democratic vanguard." If diplomacy failed, the resistance could go full tilt after the insurrectional strategy, backed by a bipartisan consensus.

The problem with this strategy, recognized from afar by the conservatives, was how not to lose control of talks. They discounted Contadora. Who could expect Mexico to condemn the principle of the one-party state? Or Panama to urge separation of the army from political affairs? There was a further problem. The Sandinistas were largely immune from the pressure of public opinion; they could negotiate with little heed for the quality or content of what was being discussed. Thus for the democratic side, the agenda of negotiations had been determined in advance, and the talks had to be entered from a position of strength.

Again, the great motor of factional strife in the Nicaraguan resistance was not principle, but power. The political differences between Cruz and Calero were not unbreachable. The FDN was not in principle set against negotiations. It had advanced several proposals since 1983 that looked much like the ones subsequently endorsed by the directorate of the Nicaraguan resistance.[25]

On the issue of talks, however, the Reagan administration was at war with itself. It was no help that responsibility for the policy was parceled out to various agencies, including State, the CIA, and the National Security Council (NSC). Victory and negotiations were goals actively and simultaneously sought by different wings (or even in the same wing) of the administration. These divisions pitted Cruz against Calero in a ferocious struggle to win over the White House, each to his own faction, because the administration's tack would vastly affect the camp of each in the resistance. In this antagonism, the gain of one was the loss of the other.

One example is the turmoil at the State Department, where only ambiguous enthusiasm could be found for the contra policy. State's prognosis on contra aid had darkened since the 1984 harbor-mining scandal. The 1985 vote, in which Ortega's flight to Moscow had weighed so heavily, had only reinforced the view that military aid in 1986 would be a fluke and should not be counted on for the purposes of policy. Serious doubts prevailed about the efficacy of the contra force itself. "There was no way they could win," said Francis McNeil, a former U.S. ambassador to Costa Rica who headed the intelligence unit at State. "The policy was unrealistic. [SOUTHCOM Chiefs] Gorman and Galvin agreed with that. Not in a million years. The only people who thought they could win were Casey, Kirkpatrick, Abrams, and North. But they were in charge."[26]

The result had been a renewed earnestness in U.S. Secretary of State George Shultz to make the best of Contadora. He had felt that the United States should consolidate its gains by easing the contra forces back into political life in Nicaragua. But the conservatives gagged at this possibility; in September of 1984 they had killed a Shultz draft treaty with an attack on its weak verification procedures. They argued it would not lead to the democratization of Nicaragua, but to a false policy of "containing" a legitimized FSLN.

This was followed by a series of purges and counterpurges, regretfully called by the victim of one of them the "Battle of the Ambassadors."[27] Curtin Winsor and John Negroponte, political appointees in Costa Rica and Honduras who had heaped scorn on current Contadora drafts, were driven from their posts by Assistant Secretary Langhorne Motley. Negroponte was replaced by John Ferch, a career official who, like Motley, took Contadora seriously. But by this time, as Roy Guttman indicates, White House communications director Patrick Buchanan was turning the contra issue into a test of loyalty to the president.[28] Shultz came under a withering 24-hour scrutiny by the conservatives. Dismayed by the high cost and low gain of his involvement, he seems to have just walked away from the Central America portfolio. After the April vote, Motley resigned. In June he was replaced by Elliott Abrams.

Abrams supported the contras and warmly opposed negotiations, which did not settle the divisions in the Department of State. In 1986, before the military aid debates, a last attempt was made to revive Contadora. Abrams took pains to stifle it. When military aid reappeared on the horizon in 1986, and with it the chance of another swipe at the Sandinistas, Ambassador Ferch was fired by Abrams—the first shot of the 1986 campaign. Ambassador McNeil, who had become number two at State's intelligence bureau and produced reports skeptical of the contras' prospects, was soon driven after him.

Conservative supporters of the contras, who now identified Shultz with Cruz, would never forgive or forget that State's position had dovetailed with that of the liberals who wanted to use humanitarian aid, along with Contadora, as a way to ground the contras once and for all. Neither would the liberals. During the debates for military aid in 1986, they howled for Shultz to retake his position of 1984, to defend Contadora, and avenge the scalping of Ferch.[29]

Under such conditions, every "How the Contras Can Win" piece in the press could be turned into an assault on Cruz. Calero had only to stand firmly for military aid and against bad treaties, and Cruz would be buried by his own friends. Cruz was on the one hand bogged down by Shultz's history of soft initiatives (which he could not but endorse because his reputation as a moderate would be ruined if he appeared more "hardline" than the administration), while on the other hand warding off poisoned barbs from the Calero camp. Cruz's advisers were mesmerized by the traps that yawned before them. To call for political reform was to confirm the troops' darkest suspicions that a sellout was at hand; not to call for reform was to surrender to the status quo.

§§ **How Calero's mastery of the FDN enabled him to assert his authority over UNO**

If the issue in 1985 was to reform the contras, Calero proved to be the most successful of the reformers. He turned the critical period of the military aid cutoff and the institutionalization of UNO into an opportunity to reassert his mastery over the movement. He suppressed the FDN's old guard, seduced the U.S. Republican Right, and paralyzed the new leadership of UNO. Calero himself became the bridge between the old resistance and the new.

The FDN was never the monolith its opponents claimed, but like UNO, a tempestuous coalition freaked by vanity and intrigue. Calero overcame all this by being the man who delivered. His success in FDN hinged not only on bringing the Nicaraguans to the Americans, but on bringing the Americans to the Nicaraguans. His peculiar skill consisted in making this appear not the trick of mirrors that it was, but an unstoppable political machine.

By dint of reliability, Calero had earned the trust of the movers and shakers of the early Reagan administration: "Uncle Bill" Casey, Jeane Kirkpatrick, Patrick Buchanan. Artful monopolization of this alliance allowed him to reduce his peers on the FDN's civilian directorate. It also gave him a clutch on Bermudez.

This position had been complicated in mid-1984, when Congress cut aid and banned official U.S. involvement in contra fund raising as well as CIA management of the program. Calero's immediate task had been to reassure the troops that U.S. aid would, in time, come again. He held the force together; indeed when the balance is drawn of his effect on the resistance, his tenacity in keeping high the hopes of the men should not be disregarded.

Good fortune soon intervened for Calero with a fabulous stroke in the form of the secret fundraising network arranged by Oliver North. Aid from the Saudis began to flow almost at once and continued to do so through 1985, eventually totaling some $32 million. The administration of these moneys was Calero's exclusive province. Even if he could not deliver the Congress, what mattered was that he could still deliver the goods. Most important to Calero, no one else could.

Calero's move to UNO, far from being a threat, was

contrived to ensure that this situation did not change. Indeed, his first coup had been to write the predominance of the FDN into the rules of UNO. This ensured that

- the constituent members of UNO retained their corporate identity
- resources appropriated by Congress for UNO would be distributed on a proportional basis, according to the resources of each entity that composed it
- the restrictions on directors' use of private funding were only pro forma.

Because of the resources facilitated by North, Calero's fiscal power—even if impaired in absolute terms from the 1983 level (and this is not altogether certain)—dwarfed all other sources available to the movement. When humanitarian aid passed Congress in 1985, the private supply network continued to operate, although it turned toward military procurement. The large share of funds allocated to FDN helped to camouflage the magnitude of the transfers that Calero received.

A fourth provision established that UNO's directorate would make decisions by consensus. In effect this gave Calero a veto over any changes to the status quo. So arose the quip that UNO was led by three, but one could outvote two.

§§   How UNO's organization comprised not a unity but a series of parallel structures that institutionalized the preeminence of the FDN

For reasons political, administrative, and military, between 1985 and 1986 UNO's leadership experienced not equilibrium but stasis. Calero continued to hold the key position between the contras and the Americans. He remained the pivot around which the military and civilian wings of the contra movement turned. He controlled the cash, the stores, the camps, and the bureaucracy in Miami.

Cruz and Robelo had hoped to gain the trust of the FDN rank and file, but this soon proved impossible. They had no point of institutional contact with the troops. Their access to the camps in Honduras was severely restricted. Even the rebel radio station remained the exclusive turf of the FDN.

Key figures in the FDN felt threatened by Cruz and Robelo. Bermudez in particular, whose otherwise blameless career in the National Guard had become a serious liability, foresaw that he would be vulnerable to calls from certain reformers for a purge of the "relics of the past." Calero's deputy in Honduras, Aristides Sanchez, also feared a reorganization of the administrative functions of the resistance (which would reduce his considerable say over a vast network of patronage), as did many others in petty and high positions.[30] Calero now set himself up as their protector.

The real axis of leadership in the resistance at this time was Calero-Bermudez-Sanchez. The relationship between the powers and the functions of these men was natural and efficient. As a senior administration official charged with implementing the policy put it, "Calero was the patron, who came in from on high; Sanchez managed the farm; and Bermudez was the peon who did the dirty work."[31]

Because the FDN's corporate identity was preserved in UNO, Calero's authority tended to radiate through a hierarchy parallel to the structures of Cruz and Robelo. Many of the civilian functions of FDN had counterparts in UNO; the relations between them were often competitive. FDN's head start stacked the competition unsubtly in Calero's favor.

Access to military information can serve as an example of how the parallel structures worked. As late as 1987, Bosco Matamoros served as FDN's representative in Washington.[32] He had a well-developed network of contacts within the CIA and the State Department. His contacts with the press went back to 1982, when he had been designated FDN spokesman. He was the exclusive beneficiary of UNO-FDN field reports and monopolized military information in

Washington. Because of this, the position of the designated UNO press secretary, Xavier Arguello, was rendered irrelevant.[33] Not only did the press secretary rarely have news for the press, as often as not what news he had came from the FDN representative's quotations in the *Washington Post*.

This situation would have been inconsequential had Matamoros competently discharged the task of representing the rebels in Washington. But this was not the case. Although charming and a purveyor of unforgettable epigrams, Matamoros was universally regarded as a living example of all that needed changing in the contras. He depended entirely on Calero's favor and competed against the FDN spokesmen in Miami and Honduras. Nominally the FDN's representative in Washington, he competed for Calero's agenda there with other Nicaraguan exiles and a host of friendly lobbying groups. They all owed much to Calero; Calero owed little to each of them.

The near irrelevance of the political wing of the movement made such a system possible. UNO existed to win aid for the FDN. FDN existed to wage war on the Sandinistas. The functional link between the political institution of UNO and the armed force of the FDN remained inert. Until quite late no efforts were made, for instance, to direct a grassroots mobilization project or a massive public information campaign or even to reach out to the exile community on a systematic basis. Often the most difficult problem facing UNO staff was how to fill the hours of a day.

Position was more important than function. UNO, like an eighteenth-century court, operated on the basis of access. Projects were judged not by what they proposed to accomplish, but by *who* presented them—who would get funds, who would meet with whom, whose position would be strengthened. Institutional channels were parceled out on the basis of loyalty; duties were rarely defined. The structure of the secretariats and their dependencies—such as international relations, law, press, and human rights—merely camouflaged what was in effect a personalized organization. UNO's institutional structure was hijacked to become an incipient cult of the *caudillo*.

This phenomenon did not pertain exclusively to Calero. The dynamics of UNO meant that Cruz and Robelo exercised their own authority in the same way. "We all sinned," concedes Arguello. "It was the way things were set up. I defended my people and Bosco defended his."[34]

But it was Calero's arbitration that always proved decisive—from preparing a press release to drafting a policy to arranging an itinerary. In every task, competition prevailed. Perpetual insecurity thus enveloped his lieutenants. The gain of one was the loss of another. Jockeying for minuscule and often merely psychological advantage in positions of influence became the rule of the day. In such an atmosphere, the safest course was to do nothing. Rife intrigue and bureaucratic ossification were the natural consequences.[35]

Such an arrangement may well have been compatible with the unity of a military corps in which obedience is paramount. But it was devastating to the credibility of a democratic movement. Robert W. Owen, Oliver North's secret courier to Adolfo Calero, was one of countless participants, Nicaraguan and American alike, repelled by this atmosphere. In note after note to North, Owen complained that "the FDN was too closed, and they believed that they could do it themselves," adding, "to too many this has become a business."[36]

The responsibility of Adm. John Poindexter and Lt. Col. Oliver North for this development cannot be overstated. Given the nature of UNO's charter, which North himself helped draft, the decision to entrust the proceeds of the secret supply network to Calero was loaded with political significance. In effect, they had handed the checkbook to the faction most inclined to disregard the rationale of UNO.

In early 1986 Owen warned North:

> If members of the [U.S. Government] think they control Calero, they also have another think coming. The

question should be asked, can and does Calero manipu-
late the USG. On several occasions, the answer is yes.
Two examples are Mario [Calero] and Bosco. For well
[over a year] USG officials have wanted to remove these
two, yet they remain. Why, because Calero won't
budge, they are part of his security; to threaten them,
is to threaten him. . . . Just one example of the lies
which are told to keep the status quo . . . Dr. Tomas
threatened to take the FDN medical corps on strike
should Bosco be booted from Washington. Tomas swore
to me this was not true and no such thought entered
his mind. . . . [37]

The dubious qualities of the fund-raising operation gave
Calero a handle on North, perhaps even on Casey, and encouraged the dark intrigues of which Nicaraguans are past
masters. North sought to take corrective steps: he tried to
remove Calero's brother Mario from the provisions loop,
sheltered the reformers, arranged for a separate income for
Cruz, and, most ambitious of all, opened a new contra front
in the south to balance the FDN. But by that time irrepara-
ble damage had been done to UNO's reputation.

The truth is that North—outwitted, overworked, and
hounded by the Left—was in over his head. This seems to
have taken its toll. By mid-1986, Robert McFarlane was
concerned enough about North to suggest to Poindexter
that he be relieved of his duties and sent to Bethesda Naval
Hospital for disability review.[38]

§§   **What little respect Nicaraguans had for UNO and
why this opened political opportunities for such people
as Cesar and Pastora**

In July, a month after the vote, Nicaraguan exiles in
Miami celebrated the passage of the humanitarian aid bill
at a reception that became notorious as a symbol of the
ineffectiveness of UNO. Arturo Cruz, Jr. acidly epitomized
the outsiders' view when he described a surreal subculture

in which the intervention of the Marines was "anticipated day-by-day":

> Homage to Calero a la Somoza, with the selfsame Master of Ceremonies, Senor Mojica, who used to wind up the band in the last days of the dictatorship: "*Somoza no te vas/te quedás, te quedás*," now organizing the *vivas* for Calero and introducing him as the "man who got the aid." The same ceremony, General Bermudez turning in the flag to Calero, and calling him "Jefe," like they used to do with Somoza. At the same time, the FDN spread rumors that if either Cruz or Robelo showed up, their presence would not be well received— that is why Calero said he could not mention their names, or the Triple A [UNO], because the public would have protested. At the end of it all, the "Shark" gushed: "Somoza may be dead, but his lessons are alive."[39]

In this context, the carefully nurtured independence of Alfredo Cesar acquired a special luster, and Pastora's calls for a "genuinely popular alternative" that "carries the true message of the revolution of 1979" began to take on a significant ring. The State Department found a new interest in Pastora, much to the annoyance of the CIA. Cesar, too, could claim to be the One True Contra. He turned away from the United States, traveling to Europe and to South America. He strengthened an alliance in Venezuela with Carlos Andres Perez, who launched his BOS into the Socialist International with observer status. Thus he obtained a valuable credential that in turn raised his stock among U.S. centrists. Ironically, a key to his success among Nicaraguans themselves derived from his judicious stoking of rumors that his BOS retained the confidence and patronage of the CIA.

Those who had held out, such as Alfredo Cesar, now seemed prescient. There was no great rally to the contra cause. The fact that everyone could agree Cruz was a nice man did not mean that people believed he would have much influence in shaping the contras or were prepared to throw their weight behind him. The FDN seemed immune to change. The administration was divided and clapped for reform with one hand only. As it emerged that President Reagan was more interested in ousting the Sandinistas than in talking to them, the reformers' own talk about negotiations was used to tarnish them in the eyes of the combatants.

Calero, true to democratic form, claimed simply to carry out the will of his followers, who were, after all, the majority in UNO. To be sure, Cruz and Robelo could hardly meet with the troops, but a rare visit to Tegucigalpa soon brought them face to face with the entrenched power of the FDN. By August, only two months after joining UNO, Cruz was depressed and threatening to resign.

On national TV, Bermudez publicly scoffed at the idea of UNO, eliciting a rebuke from Robelo in front of Cruz and Calero. "I asked him if he felt he owed us any loyalty, if he felt he was accountable to us. He said yes, but carried on as before. Cruz felt that the Americans had swindled him," says Robelo. "I myself wasn't about to quit, but there was a lot of truth in what he says."[40]

The moderates in Congress were the innocent bystanders of this indelicate scene. Overestimating their own influence, they had assumed Cruz's position was unassailable, because he commanded a key quadrant on the political grid. Aid might not come because of it, but there could be no aid without it. Thus they were puzzled when his influence seemed to wane as his purposes came closer to being achieved. The ink was hardly dry on the June 1985 bill when the old guard had moved in again to recoup its monopoly of power and prestige.

This paradox is not difficult to explain. Cruz's organizational base in the resistance was completely outmatched by Calero's. Like the cannons of the Spanish Armada, which could be fired but once per engagement, Mr. Cruz's influence was only for a day, to be trundled out for the congressional set pieces. Calero's influence was inescapably exerted, minute by minute.

This factor alone need not have sunk Cruz. By outmaneuvering Calero, Robelo, and the administration in 1987, and mounting a decisive congressional coalition behind himself, Cesar would demonstrate as much. But Cruz failed to make up for his deficiency with other strengths. He would not, in 1985, stoop to political blackmail and intimidation. Such methods would have sullied his aims. Nor would he struggle for position for position's sake, the historical sin of Nicaragua's leadership classes. Nor was it difficult to persuade him this was the wrong time to rock the boat, for above all he did not wish to harm the combatants. He also restrained his associates: "*Yo no permití el* mudslinging," recalls Cruz. Arguello agrees: "He was always holding us back from a confrontation."[41]

§§   How Cruz and Robelo sought to rally their forces, but were ineffectual in implementing reform in 1985

Cruz and Robelo both agreed that UNO was not working and that, if things did not change, they would have to leave. Shortly after his return from Tegucigalpa, Arturo Cruz met in Washington with a small group of the Democrats who had lobbied for the humanitarian aid package. He outlined his problems and over the following months developed a set of priorities that would become the agenda of reform in UNO. By October, these had been condensed to four points:

- Calero/FDN monopoly in Honduras to be broken
- centralization of all resources in the UNO directorate
- revamping of UNO's administrative structure—in particular, creation of a powerful General Secretariat to coordinate all branches of the movement

- establishment of an independent army in the south.

Cruz and Robelo outlined a plan to enter alliances with BOS and other Indian groups and to establish quasi-autonomous human rights monitors within UNO.

These proposals went nowhere in 1985. Cruz and Robelo were divided over how much or how little to ask for and on how fast a pace of change to demand. They only sank their differences at the end of the year, by which time the administration was urging them not to jeopardize the upcoming vote on military aid. Their calls for reform were timorous and ineffectual. North and Alan Fiers, the CIA official with executive authority over the program, promised Cruz that his concerns would be settled after the vote. "It was the easiest thing in the world," says Robelo. "They used to tell him, 'if you quit now, there will be no aid. And that means that the Sandinistas will win, and all of our sacrifices will have been in vain, *because of you, Arturo.*' He couldn't handle that."[42]

The moderates were alarmed when Cruz came under siege, but relieved when he did not resign. By staying on, Cruz lent UNO an image of a unity and an illusion of a balance that it did not have. The FDN's track record remained grim. Calero did little to correct a bad first impression; the intrigues that went on around him gave employment to a legion of critics who itemized the contradictions between the democratic words and autocratic behavior of UNO's most prominent leader. The faintest scrutiny exposed how marginal was the institutional base of Cruz and Robelo. Going into the glaring debates of 1986, UNO remained ill-prepared for the spotlight.

3

1986: The Real Resistance

§§ The overall situation

The Sandinistas refused to talk with the contras; with their neighboring republics, they hedged on the question of democracy. They advanced logical reasons for their position, but, because of their unmistakable totalitarian streak, lost credibility. As the Contadora initiative ran out of steam, the Reagan administration was again able to advance the military track as the centerpiece of its policy. To the contras, however, Congress was firm: no reform, no guns.

Nineteen eighty-six thus signified continuing efforts to amend the institutional character of UNO. The most important push for change, known as the May Reforms, caused the House of Representatives to eke out a $100 million aid package that included military assistance. But for Cruz, who failed to capitalize on his congressional base, the reforms were a Pyrrhic victory. Their content was directed by the administration with an eye more toward Congress than the contras. As aid began to flow, in the fall of 1986, it was evident that UNO remained firmly in the hands of Calero and the FDN. FDN, not UNO, was the real resistance. By September, Cruz again wanted to quit.

The unexpected played a sudden part in persuading him to stay. In November, the Republicans lost the Senate in mid-term elections, and Attorney General Edwin Meese III exposed the link between secret U.S. arms sales to Iran and the contras' fund-raising operation. The ensuing furor stunned the executive branch and left Calero in limbo.

To those who wished to force substantive change in the movement, this provided a rare opportunity. But they would be in an increasingly subtle competition with those who wanted to kill the contra program altogether. That conflict would be the story of 1987.

§§   How the Sandinistas anticipated a military victory in 1986, and why this gave them little to gain from a political solution to the war

In its sixth year, the FSLN looked vulnerable and isolated. Ortega blamed the economic collapse on contra damage and the U.S. embargo, but could not conceal that the tarnishing of Nicaragua's prestige abroad and rising unrest at home were of the FSLN's own making. The Sandinista revolution seemed to have reached the make-or-break point.

For all its setbacks, the FSLN still seemed to have a splendid opportunity to stop the contras in their tracks. Many, even among the contras, predicted moderation in the FSLN and a new trend toward diplomacy and a Social Democratic format to ward off President Reagan's request for military aid, expected in February. The centrist congressmen would have been happy to keep the contras on ice, a low-risk option, while giving Ortega leave to arrange political terms with which they could profess satisfaction. But three factors made it unlikely that the FSLN would pursue a diplomatic solution in 1986:

1. The internal dynamics of the FSLN suggest it had reached the limits of its tactical flexibility. Negotiations would demand a give-and-take in which Daniel Ortega would have little leeway if his faction was to remain in power.

Contadora ceased to be attractive to the Sandinistas as pressure came to stiffen its democratic terms. Under President Luis Alberto Monge, the Costa Ricans especially insisted on two of the most troublesome items for the FSLN directorate: political freedom and a national dialogue. This tallied with what the administration sought for UNO. White House and rebel diplomacy alike aimed at establishing UNO as a legitimate party to a national dialogue. The White House had had some success in finding support, at home and abroad, for the idea of a dialogue between contras and Sandinistas. Its endorsement of a church-mediated dialogue in the summer of 1985 meant that the integration of the rebels into the political process could serve as a much-needed benchmark of progress in democratization, a measure of Sandinista good will.[1] Indeed, establishing the goal of democracy as the test of a legitimate settlement was the most positive legacy of the Reagan administration's intervention in Nicaragua.

2. The contras' alliances were unstable. It was in the international arena that congressional indecisiveness took its toll. For Costa Rica and Honduras, the political cost of supporting the rebels rose rapidly; given the ambivalence in Congress, the benefits looked increasingly remote. Newly elected presidents in both countries raised doubts about their willingness to continue policies that supported the contras.

In November of 1985, Honduras had demanded that the United States send a high-level delegation to clarify its intentions with respect to the contras. Lt. Col. North himself seems to have allayed the Hondurans' fears.[2]

In Costa Rica, official doubts went deeper and could not be dispelled. Oscar Arias Sanchez narrowly succeeded Monge, his colleague in the center-left Liberación Party, in February 1986. Arias had not made peace a burning issue until late in his campaign. Few Costa Ricans were hostile to the contras.[3] Indeed, a few weeks before the election, aides of Arias's opponent had heard Oliver North crowing that, no matter who won, Monge's pro-contra policy would not change.[4] But in mid-year, after passage of the military aid bill, Nicaragua filed suits in the International Court of Justice against its neighbors for harboring insurgents and launched cross-border raids against contra camps. These actions especially discomfited Costa Rica, a self-proclaimed neutral state with no army. The Reagan administration was thus rudely jolted when Arias adopted a strict definition of neutrality and closed down the minuscule support system of the rebels' southern front.

3. The military weakness of the contras had decisively emboldened the FSLN. The high point of the rebel offensive come in August 1985 with the capture of Cuapa and La Trinidad, a mission deploying more than 1,500 combatants. The FDN was assaulted for the first time by Soviet Mi-24/5 helicopter gunships, supported by Mi-17 troop transports. Introduction of this terrifying weaponry tipped the balance of the war and put the contras on the defensive for the remainder of 1986. It forced the FDN—40 percent of whose troops had remained in Nicaragua during the aid cutoff—to scatter into small units. The lack of communications equipment (at this time the ratio of radios to men was about 1:200) obliged those who remained in Nicaragua to retreat to the mountainous northern zone and into Honduras.[5]

To seal off the troops that had retreated and destroy those that remained, the Strategic Command of the Sandinista army (Ejército Popular Sandinista or EPS) redirected its strategy. Now the strategy included the relocation of approximately 180,000 *campesinos* from the north to create free-fire zones, intensified bombardment and tactical air assaults, and extensive sowing of plastic mines along the border. By the end of 1985, the contras' outlook had never been so bleak. Joaquin Cuadra, the EPS chief-of-staff, declared that the contras were "strategically defeated." Facts on the ground did little to dispute this claim.

The opportunity the Sandinistas saw in 1986 was thus different from that which most opponents of contra aid in the Congress wanted to give them. A military victory was at hand. The alternative to making the contras' defeat complete was to enter a political process in which the FSLN would certainly lose; the question was only how much. The Sandinistas anticipated the obligation to undergo such a process sooner or later. But their objective now was to postpone it, pending the success of their military campaign.

The great risk for the FSLN was not the passage of a military aid bill. The EPS was confident that its new model of elite Irregular Warfare Battalions (BLIs) could handle a reactivated contra. That the House would resume the military aid it had cut off in 1984 was, in any case, far from a sure thing. In the Congress, the FSLN could count on a solid isolationist block that asked only for the tokens of coexistence to justify clamping down on the rebels.

Like the conservatives, the liberals were too few to have their own way. The weight of these two factions tended rather to block the legislative battle into yet another compromise "humanitarian" aid bill. The Sandinistas could receive such a bill with crocodile tears. Aid that kept the contras alive but feeble gave the Sandinistas a bogey they could hate and yet not fear. The Sandinistas' greatest concern and favorite propaganda tool was an invasion from the United States. This left the nine FSLN directors with an all-or-nothing gamble. Were it not for their willingness to take such gambles, they would never have come so far. In any event, the die was cast in their favor.

§§   Why the Republicans in the House rejected a second compromise with the swing voters and sought military aid, and how the Democratic leadership was defeated by its own devices

The administration was also compelled to seek all or nothing. That the contras put positive pressure on the Sandinistas—the basic premise of the two-track policy—had been accepted by a majority in Congress. A clear opportunity existed to reestablish the contras as the central instrument of U.S. policy. But to translate that consensus into military aid was not simple. Great contention lurked in the balance to be struck between diplomacy and force.

In the House, the contra coalition of 1985 had consisted of about 170 Republicans and 40 Truman Democrats in firm alliance and the 30-odd swing Democrats. A more hawkish proportion prevailed in the Republican-led Senate. The first two groups—the Republicans and Truman Democrats—were keen contra supporters, but their numbers fell shy of the total needed to win a military aid vote. The third group—the swing Democrats—believed that not enough of a diplomatic effort had been made to warrant resuming military aid.

The leader of the swing voters was Rep. Dave McCurdy, an urbane young Democrat from Oklahoma with an eye on his party's fast track. He had led the coalition that approved humanitarian aid for the contras in 1985. McCurdy now favored the status quo: he recognized that to abandon the contras would send the Sandinistas the wrong message, but he also felt that UNO was still too undeveloped, unpopular, uncohesive, and undemocratic to offer as a credible alternative to the Nicaraguans. He doubted they could make much headway even with massive infusions of military aid. As in 1985, therefore, his policy envisioned no active role for an armed resistance, but continued to center on diplomatic efforts to wrest democratic concessions from the FSLN.

McCurdy proposed giving $5 million "with no strings attached" to Contadora, saying, "We have had no way to judge why no progress is being made on goals that both sides have publicly embraced."[6] To create conditions for talks, he sought a halt to the war as quickly as could be achieved without dismembering the contras. They would get $50 million in nonlethal aid from the United States and would be expected to merge into the political arena. To pressure the Sandinistas and attempt to close the gap between his position and that of the administration, McCurdy proposed that a further $50 million in military aid be held in escrow "for at least" 90 days. If the Sandinistas refused "to pursue in good faith a negotiated settlement," the Congress would again vote on the release of this aid. Aid to UNO "would be conditioned upon specific internal reforms dealing with human rights and command and control of military forces."

The principal attraction of this approach was domestic. It steered between ideological tests of Left and Right, between those for whom contra aid in itself had become the issue for cheers or groans. McCurdy promised the administration that if it gave Sandinistas and contras alike an extended opportunity to make peace, irrespective of the outcome, it would find a more stable coalition on which to build long-term policy.

The contras recognized the merits of seeking a broad consensus. But timing was all-important. McCurdy's option in the short term augured defeat. It would force them to negotiate definitive terms from a position of weakness; they would have to barter concrete concessions in return for vague assurances of democratic intent. A second humanitarian aid package would be a continuing vote of U.S. nonconfidence in the military contest. Not only was it likely to sterilize, once and for all, their sanctuaries in Honduras and Costa Rica: it would destroy the rationale for the contras as an armed force.

The contras were not prepared for a political contest in Nicaragua in 1986, even had the Sandinistas been disposed to suffer one. UNO was still predominantly an army and lacked the institutional machinery, let alone the internal cohesiveness, to conduct successful diplomacy. The combatants mistrusted the politicians, such as Cruz and Robelo, who claimed to represent them. Most important, they were still confident that they could win on the battlefield; after all, they had never been defeated by the EPS.

Apart from these matters, domestic considerations also weighed heavily against McCurdy. Liberals and conservatives both complained that he was more interested in the political game within the Democratic Party and the chairmanship of the Intelligence Committee than in the stakes in

Central America. And truly, one cannot say that McCurdy was indifferent to the benefits, to his political health, of heroically exercising the congressional balance of power. In February, for example, Cruz and Robelo privately proposed to Abrams that the administration delay its military aid request until May 15, pending Contadora; Abrams agreed. But the proposal lost steam and eventually vanished when McCurdy insisted "that a delay must be a concession extracted by his people in the House."[7]

The rebels also suspected that McCurdy's promise of a consensus that put positive pressure on the Sandinistas was a red herring. The FSLN, like UNO, was incapable of reform absent pressure external to itself. Congress would certainly face the question of sanctions at some point or other. At the first lapse of U.S. resolve, the FSLN would backslide and McCurdy's consensus would break. Talks can become an end in themselves, too. The acrimony of judging the merits of military pressure would simply be transferred to the debate over whether the FSLN had been sincere, and what to do if it had not. The Sandinistas would have won a critical round, but the two-track policy might no longer be an option.

Many Democrats who now joined the Republicans to support the two-track policy believed the administration had, in effect, already given McCurdy's option a try in 1984–1985. And that option had only allowed the FSLN to sink its talons deeper into power. These 50 Democrats were the congressmen that McCurdy had to woo. But he was too flimsy on the question of democracy in Nicaragua and too vague about his readiness to sanction force. He failed to convince them that he would ever dare break with his party if it came to a vote for military aid.

For conservatives, all of this was beside the point. To them, the alternative to the FSLN was UNO. They adamantly opposed providing the Democratic leadership with a "fig leaf," the euphemism for humanitarian aid, to claim credit for providing for the contras while in fact leaving them bared to Sandinista attack. Disgusted by the administration's half-hearted request for $14 million in military aid in 1985, they warned that the United States could not retreat from its commitment to the contras without loss of face and harm to its strategic interests in the region. They echoed an unspoken tenet of the FDN's strategy—to bring things to a point where it was easier for the Americans to forge ahead rather than retreat.

Peter Flaherty, leader of a grassroots conservative group that marshaled the pro-contra coalition, noted that the Republicans were ready for a showdown. This course was risky in an election year, but the House Minority leadership thought that, even without the swings, it had the votes for military aid. Therefore it rejected the compromise:

Such a timid gesture would guarantee the failure of the President's long-term policy and condemn the Contras to a slow defeat. Tired of expending political capital for aid requests too small to make a difference, [Minority Leader] Michel and a group of House conservatives urged the President to make the $100 million request and subject it to an all-or-nothing vote.[8]

They urged a systematic campaign to bring public pressure to bear on Congress, the same way that President Carter had carried his case for the Panama Canal treaties. With little encouragement, President Reagan threw himself wholeheartedly into the fray, declaring "I'm a contra too." This was the high point of his identification with the resistance.

In March, the House defeated the administration's request for military aid. But the Democratic leadership's victory was slim. It had depended on a last-minute promise by House Speaker Thomas "Tip" O'Neill (D-Mass.) to let the swings craft an alternative proposal. As offered by Representative McCurdy in the House on April 16, this proposal provided $30 million in "humanitarian aid" to the contras and mandated direct U.S.-Nicaragua talks.

The Speaker then lost control of the House. In an astonishing reversal, McCurdy's alternative failed when liberal Democrats and Republicans combined to kill all aid. McCurdy, who thought he had struck a deal with the Republicans, felt betrayed. But some of the swing voters he led grew panicky when they were held responsible for wrecking the president's policy without being able to sustain an alternative. The administration would thus have a second chance on Capitol Hill.

§§   How these legislative developments gave Cruz and Robelo leverage that led to a new thrust for reform, and why this effort was stillborn

The changed congressional strategy underscored the enhanced purpose of the resistance. The $27 million had entailed merely the sponsoring of UNO as a prod for talks. With the request for $100 million, a difference in quantity became a difference in kind. The contras were weighing in as an alternative to the FSLN.

UNO's internal character now was subjected to searing scrutiny. In 1985, Congress had looked for unity; now it examined what unity had wrought, and it was a mixed bag. The contras' success at attracting popular support for their cause was encouraging and widely noted.[9] But the leadership, particularly in its middle echelons, showed much that was fractious and retrograde. It seemed unable to agree on a political message. The rank and file inspired sympathy, particularly the hapless Miskito Indians, but its record of respect for human rights remained depressing and testified to a lack of political discipline. The marginalization of Arturo Cruz worried many congressmen who suspected that Bermudez was still the real power behind the civilian directorate.

Cruz had natural allies in the U.S. Congress, and, after

the failure of the House vote in March, he sought to bring their influence to bear. But the forces for reform failed to connect. Part of the problem was that not even Calero's closest allies in the FDN, let alone Cruz or Robelo, knew the nature or extent of the private supply network.

It also seemed as if Cruz simply had the wrong approach. An aide to one of the swing voters, whom Cruz lobbied closely, complained that "he would talk for hours, but gave no clear picture of what was wrong, or what he wanted. The boss would have to interrupt: 'Arturo, what is the bottom line?'" An aide to Congressman Ike Skelton (D-Mo.) observed that "Cruz knew where he wanted to be, but he wasn't sure of how to get there. And that was no help to us."

The reformers' allies on the Hill noticed that Cruz and Robelo, in the presence of hostile Democrats at meetings organized by the swing voters, felt obliged to understate the depth of their differences with Calero and Bermudez, and even to cast them in a rosy hue. As Robelo frequently observed, "We're all democrats, and it's natural that we have differences between ourselves."[10]

Robelo, it must be said, could at times derive an advantage by steering an intermediate position and thus on more than one occasion undercut Cruz. His actions were as compatible with a view that the pace of reform should be cautiously managed as with the hope that the two heavyweights would knock each other out, leaving the ring to himself.

The leading pressure for reform came from Senators Nancy Kassebaum (R-Kans.), Warren Rudman (R-N.H.), and William S. Cohen (R-Me.), three Republican centrists. Absent firm guidance from Cruz, they hesitated to demand specific procedural changes. Said an aide to Senator Kassebaum, "The contras knew themselves better than we knew them. The senators were reluctant to get into a detailed prescription of how the contras should manage their affairs. They just wanted to provide some general guidelines that the contras could work out themselves. They felt the program had been micro-managed too much already."[11] To a certain extent, the senators were thus left to guess at what was needed, which hampered their efforts and made it hard for them to judge if real change had taken place.

The senators' concern had been for the contras to adopt rules that would strengthen the supremacy of the civilian authority over the military. Although they got that, their achievement was somewhat off the mark. As explained above, by 1985 Calero had skillfully asserted his preeminence over Bermudez, the field commanders, and the FDN directorate. Yet within the civilian directorate, the senators skirted the question of the equilibrium of authority. Indeed, were it not for the practical consequences of Calero's personal supremacy, in 1986 it could be said that the question of reform was settled—in the letter, though not the spirit, of UNO.

The most egregious obstacles to reform came from the administration. Kassebaum, Cohen, and Rudman, for example, sought to mandate their reforms by writing them into the text of the contra aid bill. The administration rebuffed them. Only when a White House head count revealed that the bill would fail without their votes were Assistant Secretary Abrams and Admiral Poindexter sent to Capitol Hill to find a way of accommodating their demands. The senators insisted that the language be included in the disbursement portion of the bill. Aid would be released according to a calendar tied to specific steps, such as agreement on a democratic platform, establishment of human rights monitors, and so forth. Abrams later agreed, but Poindexter objected vehemently, arguing that it would make things too complicated. He enlisted Majority Leader Bob Dole (R-Kans.) to press the senators into inserting the reform agenda in the nonbinding "policy" section of the bill.

Given such contradictory forces, it is small wonder that Cruz and Robelo believed that change would have to come from inside—that is, by agreements with the administration. Unless the agencies of the executive could agree on the shape of reform, the effort would be in vain.

§§   How Cruz and Robelo turned to the administration to diminish the power of Calero, and why this produced an inconclusive outcome

The crisis that had been simmering since Cruz's resignation threat in August 1985 boiled over after the failure of the president's request in March 1986. Calero agreed to appoint a general secretary to implement reform and coordinate the agencies of UNO. Leonardo Somarriba, a former manager of ESSO in Nicaragua, was chosen for the post.[12] Somarriba, who had a reputation for integrity, would steer a neutral course between the three feuding directors. But the Cruz people had been pushing for Carlos Ulvert, a zealous reformer.[13] They interpreted the selection of Somarriba as a defeat and blamed Robelo, who failed to support their candidate. They also grumbled at the CIA for backing Somarriba.

By early April, however, Cruz and Robelo seemed to have closed ranks behind a pair of minimum demands: majority rule on the UNO directorate and abolition of the FDN's independent charter under UNO. To the lasting resentment of the FDN, they enlisted Elliott Abrams to intervene and implement them. Abrams threatened to cut out the FDN if it did not negotiate in good faith, and he scheduled a meeting in Miami for the first week in May.

If ever it seemed possible to settle the differences of the contras from on high, it was at the Miami meeting. UNO's directors met with officials from the CIA, NSC, and State. Abrams served as the "honest broker." Negotiations lasted nearly a month, at the end of which he exulted that "more and more, the opposition today looks like what the Nicaraguan people want their government to look like tomorrow."[14]

The Basic Agreements, released in a communiqué on May 29, indeed looked like a victory for the reformers. Aside from specifically reaffirming UNO's adherence to the two-track policy, the agreements provided that

- the organization and [its] internal structures, as well as the individual members of UNO, are under the collegiate authority of the Directorate. . . . The member organizations of the alliance will place all their political, financial, and military resources at the service of UNO. . . .
- UNO is . . . governed by the principle of civilian authority over the military, respecting the line of command in each structure. . . . [15]

According to Robelo, UNO was now "stronger than ever, and this will reflect in the effectiveness of UNO's struggle both politically and militarily."[16] The May Reforms were indeed hailed by all sides as a success. But this surfeit of good feeling in itself should have sounded an ominous note, because it depended, in no small measure, on the accords' ambiguity. Most notably, the reformers reaffirmed the corporate independence of the FDN: "The member organizations of UNO maintain their own identity and framework within a pluralistic union. . . ."

The May Reforms also failed to settle the matter of majority, as opposed to consensual, rule, which Cruz had staked out as the principal issue. The Miami communiqué announced that the directorate had established a "functional and democratic decision-making procedure." In fact, a crisis had erupted when Robelo moved for the right of the minority to appeal on all cases. At length, Robelo came around to Cruz's view, but the final agreement preserved through cumbersome machinery Calero's veto power over strategy, military appointments, and major political decisions.

These provisions could well have made UNO a better movement, had they been carried out in function and not just form. As it happened, they became the substance of Cruz's case against Calero in 1987. But they failed in 1986, by leaving central control over UNO's assets unsettled. This may have been inevitable. The May Reforms, though brokered by the administration, did not produce a commitment from itself to work within UNO's institutional framework. Like the congressmen who tried to help them, Cruz and Robelo were hampered by what they did not know—the breadth of Calero's extra-institutional resources, which permitted him to be a law unto himself. As long as there was no mechanism to bring individual directors to account (before the directorate as a whole) for the moneys they raised externally, as long as the private supply network existed, as long as the constituent parts of UNO retained their corporate identity, and (most important), as long as the administration determined to keep things this way—Calero would control the FDN, and the FDN would remain the hegemonic force in UNO.

§§ How the May Reforms, by healing the breach between UNO directors, made possible the passage of the $100 million military aid bill one month later; how the reforms were soon challenged

In Congress, the May Reforms were widely noted and well received—not only for what they had accomplished, but for what they had forestalled. According to Bruce Cameron, who by this time opposed the administration's request and was working to keep McCurdy's group from splintering, "At least three of those who switched their vote did so in part because of the Miami accords."[17]

The contras were again united and lobbied heartily for the new $100 million aid bill. On June 25, 1986, the bill cleared the House, 221 to 209. Eleven votes shifted, out of the six that had been needed. Several factors were important, including the next-to-the-last gasp of Contadora over the issue of democratization, the incorporation of key parts of McCurdy's plan into the administration's bill, the discipline of the Republicans, and a noticeably more frank and conciliatory tone from the White House (the president's appeal was drafted by Bernard Aronson, the former speech writer for Vice President Mondale who would succeed Abrams in the Bush administration).

Barely a month after the military aid bill passed the House, Cruz and Robelo saw their newfound authority begin to unravel. The vehicle for the challenge was the formation of a Regional Commanders' Council that gathered the 20-odd field commanders of the FDN in an entity somewhat like the Honduran Supreme Armed Forces Council. The other rebel armies had similar consultative bodies whose powers were outlined with greater or lesser formality.

The council proposed to have a say in policy-making and to select the military leadership of the FDN. The idea originated in an old dispute between Bermudez and the field commanders. Since 1983, many combatants had asked for both the creation of cadres for the purpose of political action and education and for a greater voice in the conduct of the war. They wanted a forum to coordinate this effort. Sensing a threat to the discipline of the Strategic Command, the United States advised Bermudez to suppress the movement, but the commanders found powerful support in Calero. In early 1984, the matter reached a head when an important faction of the commanders appealed to the civilian authorities of the FDN to impeach Bermudez.

The council had not yet been formed, but Calero benefited from this continuing schism. Leaving open the possibility allowed him to check both Bermudez and the field commanders. The intemperate calls of some in the Cruz camp for a purge now drew Bermudez and the field commanders close and drove a wedge between them and Cruz and Robelo. Bermudez had always mistrusted Robelo, after the latter had attempted to displace him as chief commander during the early negotiations for UNO. The council was thus chartered in August 1986, its first act being to launch a letter of support for Bermudez as head of the Strategic Command.

Had Calero actively opposed it, such a council could never have emerged. His acquiescence was tantamount to encouragement. Indeed, key associates of Calero in the civilian leadership of the FDN, principally Aristides Sanchez and Jaime Morales Carazo, manager of FDN finances, directed the entire effort. "Calero was not an instigator of the Council, but he and Bermudez have 'tolerated' it," Robelo said. Calling it a "step backward," he lamented the challenge to the principle of civilian authority, and the evident reluctance of the FDN to recognize the preeminence of UNO.[18] By remaining aloof while the others dirtied their hands in an ugly scuffle, Calero secured his own position as arbiter of the movement. Bermudez, on the other hand, could gain stature with the troops.

Robelo led the charge against the Regional Commanders' Council. Cruz was ambivalent because he had long argued that the combatants deserved a greater share in affairs. He was not opposed to such a council in principle, but its unilateral establishment—so transparently manipulated by the FDN leadership—traduced the spirit of the May Reforms. The timing of the move raised eyebrows. Cruz thus found himself in yet another dilemma. To oppose the council would have reeked of hypocrisy and undermined the trust he had hoped to build among the troops. Not to oppose it was to surrender to Calero and the status quo. At length, Cruz decided to acquiesce, so as not to jeopardize the reinfiltration. But it seems that from this time on, Cruz abandoned all hope of reforming UNO and was simply looking for an escape hatch. According to Robelo, "He became completely ineffectual on the Directorate. He felt tricked and trapped."[19]

§§   **Parallel to these developments, Oliver North attempted to create a second army in the south to provide Cruz and Robelo a combatant base; this would counterbalance Calero and distract the Sandinista Army from the northern front**

It is useful, at this point, to take a step back in the narrative to recount the calamities that befell the Southern Front. As far as concerns the political development of UNO, this story is important, not for what happened, but for what failed to happen.

The reformers recognized that an army in the field was the most convincing sign of a deep popular commitment against the Sandinista regime. The leaders of FDN argued powerfully that their legitimacy derived from the trust of the combatants. The FDN's weight in UNO derived from its combatants' weight in the field.

Quite aside from strategic calculations, there were good political reasons for diversifying the rebels' military base. If pluralism could not be achieved within the FDN, it might be achieved outside of it, under the framework of UNO. This idea, like the light bulb, was one for which many people take credit. It struck several simultaneously, including Cruz, Robelo, Cesar, and Oliver North. For those Nicaraguans who shied away from the FDN, the challenge was to mount an operation big enough to provide a credible alternative to the northern front.

During the congressional aid cutoff, between 1984 and 1985, FDN forces had nearly doubled to some 15,000 troops. The Indians claimed about 5,000 fighters, but theirs was really a parallel struggle and could not be thought of as an alternative to FDN. Pastora claimed that by 1986 ARDE had 8,200 men, but this number played fast and loose with the distinction between soldiers and sympathizers.[20] The real figure was probably never more than a couple of thousand; in 1985 the six to eight commanders of the existing Southern Front, along with Pastora, counted on a troop of between 850 and 1,500 troops. Cesar's BOS claimed to have another 1,500, but these must have been the same men counted by Pastora. As Calero said: "Alfredo [Cesar] promised all these troops, but they must have been very quiet because that was the last I heard of them."[21] A handful of tiny *focos* had also burrowed into the jungly river border with Costa Rica and waged a classical guerrilla war, such as that of "El Negro" Chamorro—a dashing veteran who once fired a bazooka into Somoza's bunker from his room in the Intercontinental Hotel and was ransomed by Pastora's raid on the National Palace in 1978.

A front therefore existed to build upon, but it was in

disarray. At various points in 1984, efforts had been made to coordinate these units; all failed because of personal incompatibilities or lack of U.S. interest. In late 1984, a delegation representing the *foco* of about 50 men under the aegis of "El Negro" approached Sen. Jesse Helms (R-N.C.), but were ignored. In luckless attempts to provide political management now to the messianic Pastora, now to the errant Chamorro, Robelo had enough of the trappings of Maoist guerrilla lifestyle and henceforth would not stray from the political lobby.

The Cesar brothers in turn recognized opportunity in the political vacuum of the south and forged the alliance with Pastora that gave life to BOS. Much as their political astuteness was admired, the Cesars were neither trusted nor liked by Pastora's old colleagues, including Carlos Coronel (Pastora's principal adviser), Luis "Wicho" Rivas Leal and Arturo Cruz, Jr., who tried to work out a new alliance under the more tractable leadership of "El Negro." It was this combination that made contact in early 1985 with Oliver North and proposed to revitalize the south—not as just a military, but a political, alternative to both the FDN and the Sandinistas.

North leapt at the idea. His motives, as always, were complex; it is probably futile to try to untangle them. One must conjecture that a rare mixture of romance and bureaucratic intrigue stirred North: this would be his own great adventure, and he could get the CIA off his back. But more serious considerations were at hand. He was desperate to take pressure off the beleaguered columns of the northern front. The political diversion also attracted him. He was exasperated by the unreliability of the Indians and the take-us-or-leave-us attitude of the FDN. The new front even opened the possibility of giving the liberals a horse to bet on.

North promised aid on the conditions that the conspirators not infringe on Pastora's turf and that they coordinate with the FDN. In June 1985, he met with Calero and Bermudez behind the backs of Cruz and Robelo and urged their cooperation. So that things wouldn't get out of hand, the

FDN would be the paymaster. Calero could not but give his blessing. His misgivings at this transparent effort to dilute the power of the FDN were allayed by his scornful survey of the motley crew involved. As Arturo Cruz, Jr., noted:

> Of great use to them were the erratic attitudes of Pastora, Carlos Coronel's reputation as a communist, the overweening ambitions of the Cesar brothers, and "Negro" Chamorro's light-headedness. They had little trouble persuading the Americans that the South is a collection of "drunks, bums, and opportunists," and that all they can do, to please Cruz and others, is to give "Negro" a chance, even though they'll do everything they can to trip him up along the way.[22]

To some extent this is sour grapes. The Southern Front did attract some of the most attractive figures in the revolt against the Sandinistas, but they were disorganized, poor administrators, touchy, and easily distracted by intrigues. There is often a trade-off between exclusiveness and efficiency; all things considered, a key to the FDN's relative success was its selectivity. The southern front sought to forestall such a charge by becoming relaxed to a fault. Robert Owen, who served as North's representative while the front was being set up, issued chronic warnings about the people who swarmed to the affable "El Negro," seeking gain from his connection to the Americans. This throng included suspected drug-runners, thieves, profiteers, and double-agents. Advised Owen, "Tight control must be kept on the money and resources."[23] The CIA looked on the whole operation as a frightful security risk.

§§   Why Pastora, despite his legendary status, was viewed with such misgiving by those who sought to revitalize the Southern Front

The plan was to start with around 500 men, building up to a front of some 5,000 combatants by 1987. The political message would be center-left. Justice and human rights would be emphasized. A connection would be made with the Indians and with BOS. This alliance would balance the numbers of the FDN. There was even a project of "stealing" the youthful and politically inexperienced troops of the FDN from their hidebound leadership.[24] The combined front—north, south, and Atlantic—would coordinate a balanced military-political strategy against the FSLN.

Pastora, who cherished his independence, was perceived as the biggest obstacle to this plan. His maverick vision made all his alliances unstable, ultimately costing him the support of his commanders. His had seemed a friendly war against the FSLN. Pastora hoped that Managua, in its hour of need, would recognize its error, and recall him to grace. Then he would forgive all. ARDE had thus always kept the door open for an agreement. Indeed, in 1983, after three years of struggle, Pastora sent his confidant Carlos Coronel to meet with Fidel Castro, hoping peace could be made between him and the rising "pragmatic" Ortega faction. The meeting, of course, flopped, but as a U.S. official involved in the policy observed:

> The discovery of the secret mission to Cuba sent a shock wave through Pastora's followers, and through the CIA as well. How was it possible that Pastora's closest associate was meeting with the power behind the Sandinista throne? The CIA began to consider the possibility that Pastora might be a Soviet, Cuban, or Sandinista agent, sent to divide the Contra movement, demoralize its followers, and trick the Americans.[25]

Pastora soured when he saw that neither the Ortegas nor Castro had any need for him and that he would not be called back in glory. But by then the damage had been done. The United States would not trust him; nor would anyone else. Pastora reciprocated in kind. A mysterious assassination attempt at La Penca in early 1984 demonstrated that his fears were well-founded. Everybody had an interest in getting rid of Pastora: his commanders, the Americans, the

Sandinistas, the other contras. He remained, nominally at least, commander in chief of the south, but sterilized its prospects for growth.

The San Juan River, which divides Costa Rica from Nicaragua, "belonged" to Pastora. It was feared that he could sabotage the revived front if he came to believe it undermined his own prerogative. If he could not be separated from the Cesars, it would thus be necessary to isolate him from his troops. Owen advised North of this possibility in a letter of April 1985:

> Some of Pastora's field commanders are ready to join any side which will provide them with food and medicines. They have not been resupplied in at least 8 months. In fact, several of his commanders want to leave and actually aren't controlled by Pastora, he just talks with them over the radio. These include according to Poveda: Leonel, Sam, Oscar, and Navegante.[26]

Cesar was no less alert than the other conspirators for the right occasion to dislodge Pastora as head of the movement. Pastora, in turn, hoped to keep Cesar in check by retaining the card of "making peace" with the FDN, backed by Cruz and Robelo. But the obvious effort to "steal" the south reinforced the alliance of convenience between Pastora and Cesar. The one saw the advantage of having a good political manager, and the other desperately needed a base among the combatants with which to support his social-democratic credentials.

§§   How the Southern Front failed to live up to expectations; why it was nevertheless maintained as a small *foco* under "El Negro" Chamorro's leadership and eventually attracted Pastora's six commanders

Deployment of the new front gathered a good head of steam as 1985 wore on; then it fizzled. Some 150 men divided into about six camps, under the command of "El Negro."

Their mission was to move into Nueva Guinea from Costa Rica and recruit from the lake zone. The newly created UNO seemed to provide a solid institutional framework to manage the relationship with the Americans, but a fatal decision, perhaps unavoidable, was to depend on the FDN in Honduras for supplies. Deliveries came late and fell short of what was promised, breeding distrust. Calero was not a reliable paymaster; not a few suspected that this was at the request of the CIA. Close to $100,000 had been distributed between July and September of 1985, enough to set up six camps as originally planned. But it fell short of what was needed to run them properly. The cash flow crisis reached a flash point in November, when the camps threatened to disband. Calero offered only sympathy, pleading that times were tight. This rings false, considering that in August North was chuckling to Poindexter that "money is truly not the thing which is most needed at this point" and would not become an issue again until mid-1986.[27]

By the end of 1985, the veteran "El Negro" was in a pitiful plight. His political leaders began to squabble among themselves. Of the weapons expected, only half had arrived. Ammunition stacks rapidly depleted. Relations with Pastora's commanders remained tense. To complicate matters further, the new commanders, with all the good will in the world, turned out to be amateurs; Owen complained to North that many couldn't even read a map. They ventured timidly into Nicaragua and clung to the frontier. It was said they spent more time fighting the mosquitoes than the Sandinistas. As the Southern Front fell into receivership, the CIA dismissed the whole opus as another of "Ollie's follies."

Month followed month, and the Southern Front produced nothing but grief. The Americans despaired and decided to cut their losses. Carlos Ulvert, the only of "El Negro's" advisers whom the Americans trusted, came to the rescue. He argued the political wisdom of maintaining an independent south and not letting either Pastora or Calero feel they had won. In November he proposed telescoping the camps into one single *foco* of 60 to 100 men, across from the Costa Rican border, engaged in commando and special operations.

> After all, the men who remained with [Negro] Chamorro were all native to the zone, young and very dedicated, and prepared to undertake exceedingly dangerous operations. What was needed was some liquidity, and a good administrator of the military symbol of Fernando Chamorro. . . . This tactical compromise . . . is what finally saved the concept of a Southern Front without Pastora, or totally controlled by the FDN.[28]

Ulvert took over the management of the Southern Front's finances. He soon restored order and improved relations with both Pastora's commanders and the Americans. At the beginning of 1986, the new front's administrative situation had been stabilized, and it could concentrate on military activities. With the resumption of U.S. aid, its membership looked forward to a bright future.

A word must be said here concerning the cultural problem of Americans and Nicaraguans working together. The easygoing flamboyance of the characters of the Southern Front might well have translated into some sort of national symbol to inflame the imagination of Nicaraguans in contrast to the grim competence of the FDN. Witness, for all his faults, the undying image of Pastora. Dewey Clarridge, the colorful CIA officer in charge of the project, sympathized with Pastora; he realized that the legendary Commander Zero needed not just a manager, but a 24-hour psychologist. But he was a minority in the Agency. When he was replaced by Alan Fiers, a military man, matters changed. Soon the Americans tired of these people whose repeated failure made abominable the very Nicaraguan peccadilloes of tetchiness, drink, and fluency in the white lie. The Americans, by contrast, struck the Nicaraguans as arrogant, ignorant, and impatient. There was no lack of sympathy, and each side sensed the fundamental identity of purpose with the other. But in talking with those who tried to bring the Southern Front to fruition, Nicaraguans and Americans alike, one hears the frequent lament that great opportunities were ruined because of petty misunderstandings.

4

1987: A Fresh Start

§§   How the contras' military and political fortunes
underwent radical changes in 1987, and why, though
agreeing on the need for negotiations with the
Sandinistas, they sought to postpone them as long as
possible

Nineteen eighty-seven presented the contras an ironic
flip of their state in 1986. In Washington, where they had
held the high ground, they were now in frank retreat. Revelation followed revelation, building up to the joint committee hearings in Congress on the Iran-contra affair. Nervous
anticipation overtook rational discussion. At the mercy of
such forces, the contras best turned their attention to matters they could control. In Nicaragua, a more encouraging
dynamic prevailed. As American aid began to flow, the reinfiltration of rebel columns gathered speed. In 1986, Sandinista Chief of Staff Joaquin Cuadra had boasted that the
contras were "strategically defeated." By mid-1987, Daniel
Ortega himself admitted that the rebels were "a force to be
reckoned with," and that the revolution was in trouble.

This was a period for strategic review, as the contras
tried to reconcile their uncertain political fortunes with
their improved military capability. Ernesto Palazio, the

newly appointed representative of UNO in Washington, summed up the rebels' perspective in January. UNO's credibility had sunk to a nadir. For further aid, four things would have to pass: results on the battlefield, no damaging revelations from the hearings, effective reform, and negotiations.

Battlefield results were the first priority. Reform would be meaningless if unaccompanied by striking strategic advances. Nineteen eighty-seven was the rebels' year to shine on the battlefield. Their fear was that Congress would rescind the aid approved in 1986, either as a punishment or in compliance with a peace settled over their heads. The contras had until October 1 to recapture the initiative before the program came under review again. Reform and the military push would bear fruit only if deeply rooted and not easily overturned. The military push depended on U.S. aid; when it ended, the contras would have to talk terms. Time was of the essence; their diplomacy in 1987 thus aimed at buying time to gather strength, to stave off negotiations without appearing to obstruct them.

It would not be easy. Talks with the Sandinistas were an inescapable topic as Democrats charged that the two-track policy had been a sham. To the rebels, this was undoubtedly the most deadly fall-out from the Iran-contra affair. As the scope of North and Abrams's fundraising efforts emerged, the claim gained resonance that the administration had not approached either the Manzanillo or Contadora talks in good faith during the 1984–1986 congressional arms cutoff. The suspicion that the president himself authorized the connection between profits from arms sales to Iran and the contras lofted the scandal to the highest levels of government and paralyzed the administration for weeks. Echoing Watergate, the nagging doubt was "what did the president know, and when did he know it?" As the White House came under siege, speculation arose over whether Reagan, let alone his contra policy, would survive.

§§ How the contras agreed broadly on a strategy for 1987 and what that strategy envisioned

UNO's directors kept abreast of these developments, in particular the mounting pressure for talks. In January, Alfonso Robelo noted the dual nature of the rebels' strategy for 1987:

> We must keep in mind that this struggle takes place on two levels: the political level and the military level. On the political level, our most constant ally has been the errors committed by the Sandinista Regime. Capitalizing on these errors and taking the initiative at the political level, we can shortly integrate the political actions of UNO within the framework of actions taken by other Central American democrats.
> This is vital . . . I believe that if the Sandinistas were to institute reforms and return to the original plan, we would have an obligation to return to Nicaragua and test the sincerity of this reform.[1]

Cruz continued to hope for events to lead to a negotiating process as soon as possible. But even Robelo, buoyed by the troops' better chances, thought in terms of ousting the regime:

> If we strike back in the cities, close important highways, shoot down helicopters, and cut off bridges, obviously the Nicaraguan people will begin to realize that a viable option exists. . . . Upon hearing the message that the Sandinista Front is vulnerable, and can be overthrown, the people will feel free to express their repudiation of the system.[2]

The Sandinistas themselves had hitherto spared UNO a test of its collective willingness to negotiate. Peace proposals for the moment remained inchoate, allowing UNO to lavish attention on its military drive.

Military spokesman Bosco Matamoros explained that in 1987 the FDN would follow an "incremental and gradual" strategy, divided into two phases:

> The purpose in the first phase of our strategy is to regain the initiative, taking advantage of our knowledge of the terrain and of our mobility. The Resistance does not intend to engage in a "24-hour march on Managua," nor to occupy fixed positions or territory. . . . Our objective is to force the enemy to overextend its forces, and thereby weaken its front, inhibiting its access to roads and reducing its capacity to resupply and react with troops and artillery.
>
> The second phase of this strategy is to reduce the EPS to a conventional and defensive role, forcing it to defend positions and extending the war toward the Pacific and more populated areas, and increasing our operations in larger units.[3]

The first priority was to annul the huge advantage of mobility and firepower provided by the FSLN's forward attack helicopters. The contras had to reclaim the skies, which they had lost in 1985. The United States was reluctant to provide the rebels with state-of-the-art Stinger missiles, which had turned the tide for the Afghan fighters; it did, nevertheless, supply a stock of Red-eyes, which proved far more reliable than the black market SAM-7s obtained from China in 1985, some of which had even detonated on the shoulders of the combatants.

Events in the field soon changed the context within which the FSLN made its decisions. In March, during a month-long series of engagements in the Bocay region of northern Nicaragua, the government failed to reverse the infiltration of the bulk of rebel forces. The loss, through Red-eyes, of several Mi-24 helicopters in quick succession caused Sandinista pilots to fly at higher altitudes, at the expense of accuracy and intimidatory effect. By mid-year, the contra force in Nicaragua numbered over 12,000. For the remainder of 1987, they would be on the offensive.

§§   How UNO's directorate fractured when Cruz and
Calero resigned during the first months of 1987, and
why the political challenge facing the resistance
obscured the real causes of the schism

The contras got off to a rough political start in 1987.
The impasse between Cruz and Calero meant that in the
last few months of 1986 UNO's directorate had been held
together only by inertia. In January 1987, the crisis resurfaced, in a long ordeal leading to the resignation from UNO
of both men.

Political differences between Cruz and Calero received
much attention. As the *Washington Post* observed,

> Work out the politics later, Mr. Cruz and his kind were
> told, first defeat the Sandinistas. But this is precisely
> the mistake the democrats made in working with the
> Sandinistas in the 1970s to unseat the Somoza regime.
> It is what handed the Sandinistas the power they now
> abuse.
>
>   As for tactics, the FDN essentially seeks a military
> victory. The Cruz elements, understanding that such a
> pursuit can only diminish their strength, have favored
> a measure of military pressure limited to bringing the
> Sandinistas into a negotiation and restoring a basis for
> pluralism. Mr. Cruz, speaking for the external opposi-
> tion, has even been ready to delegate to what is left of
> the legal internal opposition his seat at a bargaining
> table.[4]

Matters indeed reached a head on February 15, the
same day that Costa Rican President Arias obtained the
backing of the three other Central American democracies to
present Nicaragua his proposal for a cease-fire and national
dialogue.

But Leonardo Somarriba, the general secretary of
UNO, observed that "political differences, though important, were only part of the much larger issue of the continued independence of the FDN. This was an administrative

dispute. A matter of power, if you will.''[5] Calero seems to have had little choice but to accept the substance of Cruz's policy demands, including, for example, the offer to delegate UNO's seat in the national dialogue to the internal opposition.[6] On organizational matters, however, he remained inflexible. What had emerged here was UNO's perennial failure to resolve the contradictions between unity and diversity, personality and power. Indeed, Cruz and Robelo were not the only ones to accuse the FDN of smothering its partners. On January 28, the seven commanders of the Southern Front, including "El Negro" Chamorro, broke with UNO, charging that they had received no supplies and had been the victims of a "fraud."[7] Private recriminations were much harsher. José Davila, the spokesman for the Southern Front in Costa Rica, denounced a plot between CIA and the FDN to "starve" out the beleaguered force.[8]

During a December 1986 visit to the contra camps and refugee settlements in Honduras, Cruz encountered numerous signs of the FDN's disregard for the newly restated objectives of UNO—for example, theft both petty and gross, cronyism, intimidation in the settlements, and refusal to prosecute crimes.

A glaring episode emerged in connection with elections for FODENIC, the FDN's political wing, which had been established in September 1986 along with the Regional Commanders' Council. The FDN representative, Gustavo Herdocia, according to a witness, had threatened the local refugee assembly: "Those who are not affiliated to FODENIC will receive no more provisions, nor will they be allowed to return to Nicaragua when the Sandinistas fall."[9] When the refugee assembly nonetheless went against him, Herdocia suppressed the gathering by calling in the police. According to Roberto Jiron,

> After this event the people found out that Dr. Arturo Cruz a member of UNO was in Honduras and a commission travelled to Teg. [sic] to ask him to come to Choluteca for a discussion. He said yes with pleasure

and promised to come three days later. The news spread and several meetings were organized for him. When Aristides Sanchez found out about Cruz'[s] intention, he ordered to work against that intention and sent [FDN officials] from Teg. to talk with the people.

Among them came . . . Herdocia, who menaced the people and told them that Cruz is a Sandinista and that whoever shows up will be marked as such. When they asked him why is it that Cruz is a Sandinista but is on the Directorate of UNO, he replies that that is a thing of convenience and that [Bermudez] has sent him to explain the matter.

Cruz came on the day he said and meets in various parts with great numbers of people and learns about the campaign against him. He promises that he will talk to Calero and that he is ready to resign if he does not find a solution for the problems [of the southern refugee zone].[10]

The visit to Choluteca spurred Cruz to bring matters to a head. But Cruz used up the goodwill even of his followers by indecisive attitudes and attacks that were driven more by a sort principled hysteria than by practical calculation. Bosco Matamoros observes that "Cruz'[s] American advisors failed to make the anthropological leap needed to understand that schemes developed in the air-conditioned laboratories at Harvard cannot be imposed just-like-that on top of historical, cultural, and political reality."[11]

It is true that Cruz consumed well-meaning but often unrealistic advice, which led him to squander his political capital on pathetic ventures. In January 1987, for instance, he attempted to mount a coup against the FDN. In defiance of geographic, let alone organizational, reality, he announced from the Carnegie Endowment of Peace that Bermudez was deposed as chief commander of UNO forces. Luis "Wicho" Rivas, a former associate of "El Negro" Chamorro's on the Southern Front, was advanced in Bermudez's stead. For this honor Rivas was quite unprepared and even had to borrow an olive-green sweater from the Washington office staff in order to "look military" for television. Needless to say, that was the first and last ever heard of this poor man as chief rebel commander.

Cruz removed his effects from the UNO headquarters in Miami and informed U.S. officials that he would definitely resign if the FDN continued to defy the May Reforms. Abrams was dismayed at the thought of losing Cruz just at the time Arias was mounting pressure on the United States to drop the contras; Abrams observed that "if anyone is indispensable it is Cruz." Between the February 15 and 18, yet another intensive negotiation took place in Miami.

Calero was forced to resign from the directorate of UNO. He notes that "people talked about forming a broader organization. There were serious problems, which did not seem susceptible to conciliation. And there was an institutionalized majority against me. So I quit."[12] But he remained chief of the FDN. This was unacceptable to either Robelo or Cruz, and Cruz refused to withdraw his resignation.

Abrams (whose influence in the administration was still in the ascendancy) and Frank Carlucci (Poindexter's successor as national security adviser) agreed to make the reforms stick. Cruz had demanded and at last received a rule centralizing the resources of UNO in the directorate. Now, according to Cruz, he obtained a promise that agencies of the U.S. government would abide by this rule and no longer deal independently with the FDN.[13] A tersely worded agenda of reform was drawn up, to be implemented over a 100-day period: "The Reforms shall be undertaken in two phases: (a) Reform of UNO [and] (b) Integration of BOS, MISURASATA, and other entities not within UNO. . . . "[14]

The reform agenda of UNO was divided into three categories: political, military, and financial/administrative. Most important, it observed that

> centralization of all financial resources, public as well as private, shall be the exclusive responsibility of the Directorate. This shall apply to the political as well as the military field. The Directorate alone shall be

authorized to raise private funds under the banner of the Resistance or of UNO, and the Directorate itself shall set priorities in the allocation of said funds.[15]

At a press conference, Robelo declared victory: "From now on, UNO will control the money, and with control of the money comes control of the army. . . . In the near future, the FDN will disappear as such and become a cohesive part of the Nicaraguan resistance."[16] But close observers were skeptical of Robelo's claim to have broken the FDN. Indeed, it would take some time for change to manifest itself in the resistance, and arguably it owed to many causes, including a breakup in the FDN's own cohesiveness. The problems at Choluteca were a symptom of this.

But there could be no doubt that the dynamics of UNO were changing. On February 19, Cruz agreed to stay, to help implement the reforms. By this time, however, he was a burned-out man, without concentration, will, or stamina. Within a month he resigned, declaring, "I have given all I had to give."[17]

Future historians will find a rich debate upon this point, for it is difficult not to reproach Cruz with a failure of leadership—that is, weakness at a critical juncture. On the other hand, as Calero observes, it was remarkable that he had joined the fray in the first place: "His character really wasn't of the kind needed for leadership in a war. He would have fared better in Europe, discrediting the Sandinistas."[18] Cruz's tortuous career had not been in vain. UNO was arriving at a point where it at last had a chance to be what it purported: an armed democratic force with a politically balanced civilian leadership. What was needed was to realize this potential. Yet with triumph at his fingertips, Cruz abdicated.

Cruz did not repent his joining the contras. Indeed, his resignation statement strongly reaffirmed the justice of armed struggle against the Sandinistas. But he underscored how much remained to be done; his final resignation in fact had taken place in protest at what he perceived as

foot-dragging from the administration on the matter of reforming the assembly. Regarding his most significant
achievement, the centralization of resources in the directorate, Cruz warned that

> this measure would be merely good intentions if the
> Directorate were influenced by exclusionary tenden-
> cies. The Assembly must be of the people, and the Di-
> rectorate elected by the Assembly. This leadership is
> precisely the one to press our claim upon our allies for a
> clear commitment to support the Resistance. . . . It is
> the Nicaraguans who are in positions of leadership who
> have the responsibility to make legitimate the leader-
> ship structures of a cause that is one thousand times
> just.[19]

Calero professes wonder at Cruz's behavior:

> I nearly died laughing. Really, it looked as if the only
> thing that kept him and Robelo together was opposi-
> tion to me. I had hardly resigned, but Cruz was gone.
> The truth is that he tripped himself up. He surrounded
> himself by people who didn't understand that this was
> a guerrilla army, voluntary and already established,
> that had its own way of being. He wasn't a problem
> with the troops, but more with its leaders.[20]

§§ **How President Arias slowly gathered a coalition
that, like Contadora, drifted toward breakup over the
question of democracy**

Throughout these disputes, Arias continued to seek
support for his initiative. His chief adviser, John Biehl, laid
out its premises during a low-key visit to Washington in
March 1987, soon after the plan emerged.

He placed the contras' strength in Nicaragua at only
about 5,000 men and reproached the administration for its
earlier, rash predictions that the contras were about to

sweep through Managua. According to Biehl, the contras "had not, and would not achieve significant military successes." Arias saw the contras as politically weak too. As Biehl told the State Department: "Aid to the contras passes only by slim margins—two votes, one vote, even five votes," not enough to sustain an interventionist policy.[21] To pursue it further was to court disaster.

Arias would firmly favor the democratization of Nicaragua as the cornerstone of future policy. The purpose of his plan was to leave the Sandinistas no option other than to open the door for democracy or be exposed as tyrants. The feature that distinguished the Arias plan from Contadora, said Biehl, would be a set of deadlines for clearly outlined steps to be taken in quick succession. The contras had served as a smokescreen to avoid democracy. Further aid to the contras would thus be "absolutely incompatible" with the Arias peace plan.[22]

Arias had hoped that an early summit of the five Central American states would ratify the plan by May 15. The Sandinistas rejected this, precisely because of the drift of the commitments to democratization. El Salvador and Honduras hedged by taking positions compatible with support for either Arias or Reagan. It seemed as if Arias's proposal were heading the same way as Contadora. The most the dogged Costa Rican could manage to obtain was a six-month postponement of the summit to August 6.

The contras approached the plan cautiously. In this respect, the relative calm that prevailed in UNO after the departure of Cruz underscores how little the tensions in the resistance were owing to political motives. The analysis of the Arias plan, produced in March for UNO by its Secretariat of International Relations, which tended to be dominated by the liberals, shows almost complete convergence with the attitude of the conservatives:

> [The current dialogue proposal of the Arias plan] is unacceptable for the Nicaraguan resistance: to give up our arms as a precondition to dialogue would break the

balance of power, placing the resistance in a situation identical to that of the internal political parties, whose lack of armed force has left them no choice during the last seven years but to accept the conditions imposed by the Sandinistas . . . military pressure is indispensable if we are to initiate a dialogue with the Sandinistas that has any possibility of being effective.

. . . it leaves our movement completely out of the process of negotiations, with no choice but to participate in the process of democratization which, upon signing, the Sandinistas would be expected to adopt of their own free will. Simply by signing, . . . aid to the Resistance will be cut . . . Honduras would have to expel the Nicaraguan rebels from its territory. That is to say, the signing of the treaty will mean the death of the anti-Sandinista Resistance.

We consider that without military pressure, it will be unlikely that the Sandinistas initiate a process of internal democratization, for even though this document establishes verification mechanisms, these lack coercive power. . . . [23]

Much as the rebels agreed on this, it would become a position increasingly difficult to sustain. The House approved a moratorium on the disbursement of the final $40 million of the aid package approved in October 1986, until an account had been rendered of all moneys found for the contras by the administration. The Senate killed the bill, but the contras were uncomfortably aware of the skepticism that prevailed around them.

In April 1987, Senators Kassebaum, Cohen, and Rudman assessed the impact of their reform bill, just as revelations emerged that a total of up to $97 million had been raised for the contras between 1984 and 1986. This figure was considerably more than FDN estimates of its own needs. Indeed, it appeared that more than $20 million could not be traced.[24] The three senators noted their continuing concerns about the contras:

In particular their ill-defined goals, sometimes bleak record on human rights, and inability to unify behind an agreed set of objectives or to coordinate their efforts. . . .

In the five months since the legislation was enacted, the record of implementation has been mixed. On Contra reform, although efforts have been made, the disarray and fractiousness of the Contra leadership leave grave doubts about the future.[25]

§§ Why the Nicaraguan Resistance was formed, and how it was different from UNO

To outside observers, the leadership of the contras was indeed obscure at this point, distracting from their successes in the field. For a time, UNO seemed to be breaking up into its constituent parts. The directorate collapsed into a duumvirate, composed of Robelo and Pedro Joaquin Chamorro, son of the editor of *La Prensa* whose assassination touched off the final offensive against Somoza. But under the surface, matters were being resolved, restoring the community of interest among the anti-Sandinistas.

Two weeks after Cruz's departure, for example, the commanders of the Southern Front resolved to return to the common front, "since we are at last receiving military aid in the depths of Nicaraguan territory, [and] the structures of UNO are being revamped."[26] As early as January 10, the political, if not the practical, obstacles to a new union of rebel groups had been smoothed in the Democratic Charter signed by the leaders of UNO and BOS.

Calero's plan to seek reelection at the fifth UNO Assembly, scheduled for early May, would have isolated Robelo, because Chamorro was widely regarded as under Calero's influence. Yet Calero's position had become vastly complicated, not only in UNO, but within the FDN. He felt threatened by close associates in Honduras, on whom he had become too dependent. The mistrust was reciprocated:

Sanchez and Bermudez believed that Calero had lied to them about the private supply network and was trying to suppress them. The charter confirmed their suspicions that as in 1985, he was prepared to make overtures to the Left, strengthening his own position at the expense of theirs.

The field commanders' council now backfired on Calero, as Bermudez encouraged them to nominate Aristides Sanchez to the directorate as the combatants' representative. By one stroke he gained an ally on the directorate and rid himself of competition in Honduras. This move made the break between Calero and his erstwhile deputy complete and chilled relations between Calero and Bermudez.

The assembly was not without surprises. Alfredo Cesar, who had been waiting for such a moment, merged his BOS with UNO, chartering a new organization billed as the Nicaraguan Resistance. Azucena Ferrey, a well-known leader of the Christian Democrats, dramatically left Nicaragua to take her seat on the new directorate, advertising the subterranean links between armed resistance and internal opposition.

Calero had bargained on installing his close ally Alfredo Sacasa as a director, cutting out Sanchez. Such an action would have allowed him to line up with Chamorro, and *sub rosa* with Bermudez, to thwart Robelo and Cesar. Instead, Calero now faced the prospect of a Cesar-Robelo-Sanchez axis, in which Bermudez could be the balance of power. Ironically, balancing the civilian directorate now served to raise the stock of the military commander, who was immediately reconfirmed in his post. The reversal of Calero's fortunes was widely noted. His jealously guarded connection between Washington and the combatants was no longer a monopoly. The exalted would-be *caudillo* was suddenly just one more lobbying politician.

The new assembly, which codified the reforms Cruz had sought into the statutes of the Nicaraguan Resistance, was itself an instance of the effort to accommodate the broad range of democratic opinion. The thorny issue of political equilibrium was resolved by recourse to principles of repre-

Unaware of this development, the contra directorate had arrived in Washington to lobby for continued military aid. But at a meeting with the Republican House Leadership, House Minority Leader Michel continually interrupted their efforts to ask whether the directors would be willing to return to Nicaragua if the Sandinistas agreed to restore democratic freedoms. As for military aid, Senate Minority Leader Robert Dole told them that they would probably have to give time "in order to strengthen the President's hand."[30]

Although rumors of a deal had abounded, the unveiling of the Reagan-Wright plan on August 5 caught the contras by surprise. The plan was the first great test of the cohesiveness of the newly structured resistance. Indignation brought the leaders together. They all felt that the administration had treated them shabbily by not keeping them abreast of its dealings with Wright. The Sandinistas had been well briefed; indeed, the Nicaraguan ambassador had had a hand in hammering out the details with Wright and Michel. The rebels nonetheless recognized that their only choice was to endorse the initiative. "The plan isn't perfect," said Robelo, speaking for the directors, "but we can work with it."[31]

In Congress, the wings of each party scorned the plan. The Left was enraged by the Speaker's tacit agreement to hand the president a vote on military aid if the Sandinistas failed to respond, and he was subject to heavy sniping. Rep. Jack Kemp (R-N.Y.) denounced the plan with scorn as a thinly disguised sellout.

Some contras, not unhappy to make a virtue out of necessity, now had the chance to establish the two-track policy once and for all. Unafraid to enter the political arena if guaranteed a fair contest, they had feared that the administration would take the advice of the ultraconservatives and force the military issue (as it had in 1986)—either to put the contra problem behind itself or to pin the blame on the liberal Democrats.

Such was not the case. The administration was eager to recapture the middle ground and not about to play "Who

sentativeness rather than proportionality. The assembly was thus composed of 54 representatives, who were divided into nine equal blocks of six to be filled according to the procedures of each sector of the resistance.

All contra forces, agencies, and resources fell under the collective authority of the directorate. A pair of directors were to hold the military portfolio on a rotating basis, which, in principle, abolished the autonomous character of the FDN. In practice, the administrative convenience of many of the old arrangements caused them to linger. In a new political charter, the Patriotic Covenant, the resistance outlined specific provisions designed to guarantee a democratic future for Nicaragua. Symbolically important was a commitment on the principle of nonsuccession in power. The directors and the commanders of the war fronts were to be barred from the provisional junta, which was envisioned as succeeding the Sandinista regime. Members of the junta would be barred from being candidates for president or vice president in the first general elections. Such rules were an open invitation to the internal opposition.[27]

The contras still had to overcome the ingrained skepticism of years of disregarded reform promises. But soon, unmistakably, things began working differently, and a different atmosphere actually prevailed. Honduras was thrown open to the new directors, who mingled freely with the combatants. Relations between the military commanders and the civilian directors were smoothed. Duties were redefined, and lines of authority clarified. The parallel structures that had plagued UNO withered away. Intrigue did not erode institutional channels but rather was shunted through them, as in any well-established political entity. As all this took place, there was a burst of renewed confidence in the leadership of the resistance. Cordiality became the rule between factions that only weeks earlier had been at each others' throats. Bosco Matamoros and Xavier Arguello embraced.

That the Nicaraguan Resistance was billed as a new organization was largely a sound public relations move, for it was based on reality, not just appearance. Somarriba, the UNO secretary general, points out that "insofar as reform was necessary, or had taken place, it was in fact all worked out before the Nicaraguan Resistance was chartered."[28]

As an example, one can point to the perennial problem of authority over the moneys of the resistance. One of the first targets of reform was the scandalous contra fund-raising. The FDN's direct-mail operation, the Freedom Fighter Supply Fund, had been set up with the help of Carl "Spitz" Channel and entrusted by Calero to his lieutenants in Washington. Ostensibly its revenues, which arrived in the form of small contributions, served to amortize a $2 million debt acquired by the FDN in Honduras during the aid cutoff. But the operation was grossly mismanaged. It is impossible to describe the disorder and filth in the office where the returns were processed. Checks were scattered across the floor, mingled with the letters of well-wishers urging that their contribution be well used.

In March, the directorate deposited this mess with Somarriba and Ernesto Palazio, the Washington representative, an independently wealthy lawyer with a well-deserved reputation for honesty.[29] Palazio hired professional accountants to restore order and help manage the new 501c(3) Nicaraguan Resistance foundation established to coordinate fund-raising.

Calero continued brazenly to violate the charter by re-establishing ties with Channel's associates (who by now had pleaded guilty to tax fraud) and authorizing them to solicit funds in his name. The directorate reacted strongly and placed notices in various newspapers declaring that the Washington office was the sole body authorized to collect funds in the name of the Nicaraguan Resistance. But Calero was not deterred; as late as August 1988 he was soliciting funds independently of the directorate. The dynamics had changed, however. He no longer enjoyed the support of his old FDN associates or even of the administration. A rebuke from House Republican Leader Robert Michel at a meeting between the directorate and the true believers in Congress dramatically emphasized Calero's isolation.

§§ **Why the president and the speaker of the House sought a new agreement on the two-track policy, and how the rebels met the first test of their willingness to negotiate; why the initiative passed from the U.S. government to the Central Americans, as the Sandinistas unexpectedly subscribed to the Arias plan**

The Iran-contra hearings produced an electric, if confused, impression on the U.S. public. The hearings did not settle the debate on contra aid, but helped clear the air of much that had been worrisome: the depth of the president's involvement in activities that seemed banned by law, the charges that a secret cabal had overturned the normal process of government, and fears that the contra policy had spun out of control. After an exciting summer, Washington began to slide back into routine.

Indeed, when the hearings closed in July, the rebels breathed a sigh of relief. Three of the four conditions outlined by Ernesto Palazio at the beginning of the year had been met. The contras' conservative backers claimed to see a surge of popular support after North's testimony and urged the White House to strike boldly for military aid before Congress broke for its summer recess. But military aid was not in the cards.

Shifting polls had not changed the vote in Congress. Under Chief of Staff Howard Baker, the president was served by people who shied from confrontation. The domestic risks of forgoing a consensus no longer seemed worth the rewards. When it became evident that a bill carrying military aid would fail, Tom Loeffler, a former Republican House member from Texas, was sent to work out a deal with House Speaker Wright. The president wanted the Speaker as his principal in a new diplomatic duel. The Sandinistas would have 60 days to cut off Soviet military aid and restore the democratic process. If the Sandinistas talked to the contras, the United States would talk with them. The Speaker agreed on condition that the administration withhold its request for military aid. The deal was hammered out by the first week in August.

Lost Nicaragua?" As expected, the center welcomed the initiative. The Reagan-Wright plan promised to strengthen the center in the resistance as well (if it did not kill it).

Just as the divisions in the administration had helped divide Cruz and Calero, the divisions among the Republicans fueled a rivalry between Calero and Cesar. Each vied for support from Bermudez and the combatants. Dark rumors of "done deals" were part and parcel of this contest. Calero, anticipating the failure of the Arias plan and standing firmly for a new military package, poised himself to be the champion of the hard line. Rep. Kemp and a coalition of the Right served as Calero's base, placing strong pressure on the Republican House leadership to ask for the incredible figure of $270 million in military aid. Cesar worked with centrists led by Rep. Mickey Edwards (R-Okla.), the party designated point man on contra aid, to maintain a negotiating stance that would keep the bipartisan coalition intact and ensure that the anticipated failure of the accord be blamed on the Sandinistas, not on the resistance.

Events overtook the contras yet again. As scheduled months earlier, on August 6 the Central American presidents gathered in Esquipulas to reconsider the Arias plan, this time with Nicaragua present. Faced with the rigorous terms of the Reagan-Wright plan, Ortega leapt for the relatively diaphanous agenda offered by Arias. The Speaker vindicated this decision by declaring, in a highly controversial move, that his agreement with Reagan had been superseded by the Arias plan.

§§   How the Sandinistas' ambiguous compliance with the plan led to the emergence of a tacit bargain between the resistance and the Congress, in which the contras would be sustained as long as they continued to negotiate reasonably

The directorate took some time to respond to this new, more complex challenge. They feared the obvious: the Arias plan would serve the Sandinistas as a smokescreen to destroy the resistance while evading its democratic demands. To forestall this possibility, they delayed acceptance of the plan until obtaining, on August 21, the support of Salvadoran President José Napoleón Duarte for an interpretation of the accord that demanded the resistance be included in the national dialogue.[32]

A deeper concern underlay the unity of the resistance. Nicaragua's perfidy-marred history is in no small measure the product of leaders' breaking faith with followers. Calero's unyielding commitment to the military contest had served a vital function in this respect; he had earned, by deeds, the confidence of his men. The new directorate had to persuade the combatants that no dark pact was in the making. A strong sentiment prevailed that the resistance had relied too much on the United States and that this was the time to defy the odds and carry on the struggle alone. Perhaps 3,000 to 5,000 troops were ready to carry on the fight rather than depend on the bona fides of either the Sandinistas or the United States. These fears needed allaying if the political discipline to carry out a successful cease-fire negotiation were to be maintained.

Although wary of appearing to work against the peace plan, the directors were concerned that the $100 million package would expire on September 30 without consensus on the shape of a new one. The political consequences of an interruption in U.S. support would be grave, but practical concerns were even more worrisome. Although Bermudez disposed of sufficient materiel to sustain combat at current levels for another three months or so, he depended on U.S. food drops to continue to operate in the Sandinista-cleared free-fire zones. If a cease-fire were not arranged, he would be forced to a disastrous retreat.

Consequently, within a week of their dialogue offer, the directors also proposed a restricted aid package. As Alfredo Cesar explained:

This new aid would include a humanitarian component which would be immediately and continuously available, and a lethal component which would be kept in escrow, and would only be disbursed if the regime of Dictator Ortega does not comply, on November 7th, with the signed commitments of the peace plan.

If the democratization of Nicaragua is undertaken and thus peace is achieved, which is the objective of the Nicaraguan Resistance, the lethal component of the aid kept in escrow would be used to facilitate the reincorporation of the rebel forces into the normal life of the country, and on food for the people of Nicaragua.[33]

This proposal was ignored, but the Arias plan nonetheless soon came to grief. Deadlines were postponed, then ignored. The Sandinistas did little more than to restore civil liberties that they could easily suspend; they argued that as long as the United States and its allies continued to aid the contras, they (the Sandinistas) were under no obligation to comply with the plan. As deadline after deadline lapsed, pressure mounted from Rep. Kemp for the administration to engage in another all-or-nothing push, this time for the $270 million in military aid. Abrams and NSC Latin America specialist José Sorzano were the most vocal supporters of this strategy. A wary Shultz restrained them. Circumstances in Nicaragua remained highly ambiguous; Costa Rica led the other four countries in hesitating to accuse the FSLN of bad faith. Indeed, in October, El Salvador and Honduras both asked that the administration postpone its aid request until after January 7, 1988, when a new Central American summit was scheduled.

Rep. Kemp's efforts proved fruitless, but the Sandinistas' deliberate ambiguity prompted Congress to pass, on September 30, 1987, the first of five short-term continuing resolutions for humanitarian aid. The allotments were sufficient to meet the contras basic needs into early 1988, without much diminishing their fighting capability.

Thus was set the pattern for a tacit bargain between the resistance and Congress. As long as the rebels proved willing to negotiate in good faith, they would continue to receive support. Alfredo Cesar in particular, who sought to be identified as the chief negotiator of the contras and the champion of the two-track policy, staked his reputation on this quid pro quo.

§§   How, at the end of 1987, the contras felt they had gained the political initiative

By the end of 1987, the contras were shifting into high gear. The first phase of the military objectives postulated by Bosco Matamoros had been attained. On the political side, they had met three of the four conditions outlined by Ernesto Palazio: they had seized the initiative in Nicaragua, were confident about the success of their reforms, and felt vindicated by the Iran-contra hearings. The last condition, willingness to talk, seemed to be heading nowhere because of Sandinista intransigence.

The contras were displaying an unprecedented degree of cohesiveness and political flexibility; they parried the Sandinistas' political and military strokes with ease. In October, for instance, the FSLN launched an intense psychological operation to pry the rebel troops from their leaders, bombarding them with leaflets that urged acceptance of the amnesty, and showing them pictures of Cardinal Obando with Ortega and Calero. Some read, "We've settled everything; come home now," and others read, "Your choice is simple: work, peace, and food, or death." The combatants themselves spurned the proposal as an affront to the peace plan and their institutional integrity; they referred the Sandinistas to the contra political leadership as the proper partners to a negotiation. That month, the operation "Comandante David" combined over 3,000 rebels to cut off the Rama road, Managua's lifeline to the Atlantic.

The Sandinistas' international position also was decaying badly. Major Roger Miranda Bengoechea, the right-hand man of Nicaraguan Defense Minister Humberto Ortega, defected with the blueprint of a militia buildup to an astonishing 600,000 troops. Subsequently, Humberto Ortega himself confirmed the plan. That it seems to have been drafted *after* the signing of the Esquipulas II agreement raised a firestorm in the Central American capitals. As President Arias sank in the polls, the Gallup affiliate in Costa Rica found that 77 percent of Costa Ricans thought the Sandinistas would not fulfill the peace plan. Sixty-four percent favored U.S. military aid to the contras.[34]

On December 5, the Democratic Coordinator of the internal opposition asked for the transition to a new regime:

> At this juncture, no recourse remains but to declare the Sandinista regime absolutely incapable of governing the country. We demand the transition to an authentically democratic form of government. We believe this transition can be accomplished within the framework of the agreements of Esquipulas II:
>
> 1. Granting a general amnesty. The previous measure extended indulgence only to 985 prisoners, while over 9,000 prisoners remain in the jails.
> 2. Concerting a genuine ceasefire. This can be achieved only on the basis of dialogue with the armed resistance, which, added to the dialogue of the political parties, should lead to a government of National Unity.
> 3. Lifting the State of Emergency, the necessary condition for the exercise of political pluralism and freedoms of expression, association, and movement.
> 4. Engaging frankly in the national dialogue. That today it is at a standstill is the Government's fault.[35]

The national dialogue, created by the August 7 agreement, reached a terminus when demands for constitutional reform supported by 14 of the 15 internal parties were rebuffed. These reforms would have effectively ended the FSLN's control of the army and the state. Even the traditional Communist Party denounced the FSLN. Not only was an unprecedented degree of unity being shown by the internal parties, but Daniel Ortega warned on December 16, "The distance is quickly closing between those Contras who are armed and those who do not have guns in their hands." He vowed that "even if the people became deranged" and the FSLN were forced to relinquish the government, it would "never give up power."[36] Such intemperate remarks elicited worldwide condemnation.

The contras now took the offensive in demanding a part in the national dialogue. In November, Ortega had been forced to reverse the long-standing FSLN policy of opposing any recognition of the "mercenaries." Only days before, the hard-line Commander Bayardo Arce had declared that talks "would never take place, anywhere, in any form, directly or indirectly."[37] The FSLN now agreed to an indirect mediation, directed by Cardinal Obando, but throughout November and December it effectively postponed any movement toward this possibility.

As the year closed, it was no longer possible to evade the fact that the Sandinistas had failed to respond adequately to the peace plan. The question was what to do next. The *New York Times* bemoaned the "nasty choices":

> How can Congress send more guns to the Contra rebels? That would flagrantly violate the new Central American peace plan, which forbids all foreign aid to insurgents. Then why not cut off all Contra aid? To do that, before the Sandinistas have complied with the plan, would remove the one pressure point that seems to burden President Daniel Ortega and the other comandantes.[38]

As pressure to open talks built up on the government, the rebels stepped up the pace of their military effort. The scope of their operations had grown steadily more ambitious since the October "Comandante David" assault. The largest operation of the seven-year war took place in December. The contras claim to have massed over 7,000 troops for a four-day strike at the gold-processing centers of Siuna, Rosita, and Bonanza. "The Sandinistas were reeling," observes NSC adviser Sorzano. "The Contras were hitting them from all sides, and they were simply failing to respond."[39]

5

1988: A False Start

§§ How the contras seemed to have recaptured the initiative for a new military aid request; why the vote in February, far from evoking a consensus, triggered another all-or-nothing showdown

Entering 1988, the contras were more optimistic and united than ever before. They had attained the first objective of any guerrilla movement—to be recognized as a legitimate representative of the people. Their problems of credibility were behind them; they could focus on the present and the future, rather than dwell on the past. As the *Washington Post* observed on January 2:

> The resistance is toughening its bargaining terms. Its priority is to gain Sandinista acknowledgement that it is a proper partner to a political deal. Certainly the rebels are entitled to a political role. They are currently in an improved strategic position to claim such a role. The considerable popular support they have mustered belies the charge that they are exclusively a mercenary caste still dominated by elements of the discredited Somoza past.[1]

On the same day that the administration announced it would ask for a $270 million military aid package for February 3, the Central American presidents reconvened in Costa Rica to review the Arias plan. The plan's future looked bleak.

Thus Ortega surprised everyone when, urged by President Arias and a Democratic embassy from the Speaker, he acceded on January 16 to direct cease-fire talks with the resistance, to lift the state of emergency, and to restore civil liberties. He pledged to fulfill the original Esquipulas agreement "unrenounceably and unalterably" and "without hesitation or deviation."

The effect of this was to make more mushy the ground under the swing voters. On January 21, a group of 20 representatives led by McCurdy urged President Reagan to delay his request for military aid:

> We are convinced that Nicaraguan President Daniel Ortega is, for the first time in nine years, being forced to recognize and pay more observance to the democratic principals [sic] on which his regime was empowered . . . if you believe you absolutely must come forward with a request for additional aid, we urge that all aid be non-lethal and placed in escrow. . . . [2]

But McCurdy was in fact taking a leftward swing. He had dismissed as "nothing new" the information provided by defector Miranda and demanded that the administration enter security talks with the Sandinistas and with the Soviet Union. The latter request was sparked by a cryptic comment by General Secretary Mikhail Gorbachev to President Reagan during the Reykjavik summit.[3] Another influential swing voter, Jim Slattery (D-Kans.), wrote to the Speaker and observed:

> Clearly the Contras have provided some pressure on the Nicaraguan government. . . . Ortega should be given a chance to prove if he means what he says, but the Con-

tras cannot be abandoned on the strength of his word. It seems to me that the peace process can be served by keeping the Contras in the field until the terms of the peace plan have been fulfilled.[4]

Slattery nevertheless stood firmly against military aid as long as a diplomatic initiative of any sort was on the table. He tried to persuade the rebel directorate to endorse an alternative proposal for $32 million in food, shelter, clothing, and medical supplies, to be "delivered to the Contras in cease-fire zones within Nicaragua." Slattery envisioned a coalition of 250 to 300 votes for such a course, if the rebels would only endorse it. To a dismayed Alfredo Cesar, he said, "The zones will be your great opportunity to show people what you're about. People will flock to the zones; you'll be feeding them there."[5]

The legislative arena was being set for another showdown. Moderate Democrats who supported the contras sought to avert another bruising all-or-nothing vote and proposed that the president whittle down the military portion of his aid request and attach it to an escrow mechanism that would include consultation with Congress.[6] As the package took shape in the days and hours before the vote, the administration sought to factor in these concerns. But it was not seeking a broad consensus. According to a senior administration official charged with crafting the policy, two objectives were sought: to meet what the traffic in Congress would bear and to meet the needs of the Nicaraguan Resistance *for victory*:

> We were going for the kill. In January, the Contras were driving very hard, and the Sandinistas had lost their ability to contain them. At that level of fighting, according to our intelligence estimates, they would have won by the end of the year. They did not need further heavy supplies, just ammunition and air support. Hence the apparent small size of the "military" portion of the package, $3.6 million. But when one took into account the aircraft support services, humanitarian

aid, logistics, etc., the package added up to some $57 million, almost $200 million on an annualized basis.[7]

Precisely against just such disingenuity, Rep. John Spratt, Jr. (D-S.C.), one of the more conservative of the swing voters, rebelled. "I couldn't put up with Elliott Abrams and the administration cramming another military package down my throat while there was still a peace plan on the table."[8]

The administration put all its eggs into this basket. Hours before the vote, the directors nervously asked the secretary of state what would become of them if the vote failed. Shultz replied with Delphic equanimity, "You shouldn't even think of it." But the fatal blow to the contras' hopes for a bipartisan package had been struck days before, when in response to Ortega's move, the House Democratic leadership returned to Tip O'Neill's strategy of 1986 and promised McCurdy, Slattery, and the other swings a vote on the package of their choice if they defeated the president's request first.

Hours before the vote the president offered to consult with Congress on the release of military aid. This seems to have won over at least four of the swing voters. But it was too little, too late. The administration's lack of credibility came back to haunt it. Ortega's last-minute promises carried the day. Military aid failed, 211–219. The initiative again passed to the House Democrats.

§§ **How the contras tried to shape the new package, and why the House voted against the Speaker**

The grim memory of 1984 now loomed before the contras. Failure of the February 3 package came as a particularly rough blow to Cesar, who had lobbied fiercely for military aid. His career had been built on the "tacit bargain" that, if negotiations were carried out in good faith, Congress would continue to support the resistance.

As Shultz's reply had suggested, the administration had no back-up plan. It took a wait-and-see approach and disregarded an invitation from the Democratic leadership to join in an effort to provide the contras with "strictly humanitarian aid."[9] But the Republicans were of two minds over how to proceed. Some stood adamantly for nothing less than a full military aid package; if the Democrats failed to provide, then they should take the consequences for their action. But there was also broad feeling in favor of seeing what the contras could work out with the Democrats; if they found terms with which they could profess agreement, so much for the good. As Republican Senator John McCain (R-Ariz.) told Calero and Cesar, "If you like it, we'll like it. If you don't, we won't." Thus, for once, the contras felt free to design their own aid package and not just to lobby for what the administration had disposed.

That the contras were prepared to undertake such a complex lobbying task underscores the degree to which they had evolved into a sensitive political body. Lack of a bureaucratic apparatus in itself would have made such a course unimaginable in 1985. The rebels' fractious impulses remained a problem (though much mitigated), for as in the period immediately following the Reagan-Wright plan, divisions in the Republican ranks continued to exert a centrifugal effect on the contra leadership. Calero sided with the administration in favor of aloofness. Cesar shuttled between the Speaker's rooms and the House Minority leadership, seeking a compromise package. He dragged the breathless Sanchez all over Capitol Hill, like a human shield, to ward off rumors that he had lost the confidence of Bermudez and the troops.

Cesar hoped to work out with the Democratic leadership a strong nonlethal package that Bermudez could bless and the Republicans would support. His belief was somewhat justified that, if negotiations failed, the tacit bargain was not yet dead and he could lay the ground for continuing the two-track policy in the future. Given the reserves of the resistance, a package that included air drops and communications equipment and did not bar acquisition of previously authorized equipment might allow the combatants to hold out in a defensive position and give some leverage in cease-fire talks. It was essential to keep the contras intact and with high morale as a military force. The basis of Cesar's proposal therefore was the following:

1. A credible U.S. government delivery system
2. An expedited vote in the month of June [1988] reviewing the overall situation
3. Communications equipment to maintain command and control of our forces.[10]

To work out the package, the Speaker appointed a task force of 10 Democratic representatives. Although evenly balanced between liberals (who felt no obligation to the contras beyond ensuring their safety as refugees) and swings, this action suggested to Cesar a desire in the Speaker to see a favorable nonlethal package. Indeed, it was not against Wright's interest that a package satisfactory to the contras emerge from the task force. Having killed the president's package, he was obliged to come up with a robust alternative of his own.

Cesar was acutely aware that a majority of Democrats were eager to box him into a false negotiating position as had happened to Cruz, which his rivals would interpret to the troops as surrender to the FSLN. His space to maneuver was thus dangerously circumscribed. Calero worked with Rep. Kemp for a stronger "mixed-deliveries" package that would be presented as an alternative if the Democratic package failed.

The Speaker had difficulty concealing his nervousness. A few days before the showdown, Deputy Whip David Bonior (D-Mich.) had solicitously sounded out one of the resistance directors whether the White House could bring the Republicans along if the Speaker's package fell through, "so that the Contras would not be totally abandoned."[11] This was a transparent ploy to see whether the Republicans had enough votes to defeat the Democratic package. The test of Wright's leadership would be to whip enough votes back from his own party to carry his package. Conservative Democratic supporters of the contras were essential to this strategy. The liberal Democrats might well mutiny, and as Tip O'Neill's embarrassing setback had shown in 1986, the remainder was too slim to carry a vote in the face of opposition from the contras' faithful friends.

A week before the vote, the Speaker's task force thought it had reached a deal with Cesar. But on the day the Democratic package was to be presented, Cesar bailed out. The House Republicans advanced their own proposal, and the Speaker's ambitious policy began to falter.

It remains unclear whether the task force merely thought it had a deal or if Cesar had struck a bargain that he could not deliver. One way or another, at the last minute pressure was brought to bear on Cesar from the Right. A rumor (of the sort to which Cesar was particularly vulnerable) emerged that he was "selling out" for a false package. In a panic, he notified the swing voters that his position was being misrepresented "by other members of the Congress and in the Administration." He restated his proposal in terms the Democrats would not accept.[12]

One of the minor mysteries of the story concerns the origin of the "shot in the dark" that made Cesar recoil. Rep. Spratt, a member of the Speaker's task force, believed an agreement had been reached with Cesar and even with the moderate Republicans. He recalls discussing the contents of the package with Colin Powell, the national security adviser, "and he said it sounded O.K." But Powell certainly did not give the package an endorsement; he and Shultz in any case parted for the Moscow Summit that week, leaving their deputies, Abrams and Sorzano, in charge. Spratt blames Abrams for spoiling the deal. Sorzano disagrees that any deal was made, noting that the administration was unanimous in considering the Democratic package unacceptable.[13] There can be no doubt that the Republicans held out a better deal; the contras took it, to the chagrin of the Speaker.

The two packages came remarkably close to one another by the time they were presented on February 24. The Republicans would have allowed $22.5 million for a range of nonlethal items, including helicopter parts and jeeps, whereas the Democratic package provided $16 million strictly for such humanitarian goods as food and medical supplies. The Democrats specifically banned the CIA from management of the deliveries, but this was for public relations' sake. They eventually caved in to Cesar's request that, for the sake of combatant morale, these functions be taken over by the Department of Defense rather than some refugee agency. As one of the task force Democrats snorted at the time, "It's just a question of some guy moving his rolodex from one office to another; I wouldn't give a damn but the liberals won't budge otherwise."[14]

A critical difference concerned future authority over the decision to renew contra military funding. The Republicans would let the president have a second vote any time after April 15. The Democrats would not yield this authority. Their vote trigger was to be a report from the House Intelligence Committee (controlled by the Democrats), and it would be the privilege of the House Democratic leadership to introduce the new bill.

By this stage, the issue had less to do with Nicaragua than with domestic matters. Here the all-encompassing issue of who should be in charge of U.S. foreign policy was being decided. The executive branch bravely defended its prerogative. Wright, equally determined to mount the challenge, pushed ahead for the second legislative showdown in a month.

On March 3, Democrats voted in favor of the Speaker's package by a narrow majority. Because of a House rule, this vote killed the Republican alternative. But the archliberals felt betrayed by Wright's double-dealing, and the contras' 40-odd Democratic supporters refused to vote for a package the rebels would not endorse. On final passage, usually a pro forma repetition, both factions joined the Republicans to kill the Speaker's bill.

Arias's complaint that "aid to the Contras passes by only one vote, two votes, even five votes, but not enough on which to sustain a policy" now landed on its flip side. Wright's policy, like that of the administration, was wrecked by a handful of votes. Visibly shaken, he conceded defeat by quoting Will Rogers: "I'm not a member of any organized party, I'm a Democrat."

§§ How a vacuum prevailed in Washington, passing the initiative to the Sandinistas and leaving the contras in limbo

Peace would have its chance. U.S. aid to the Nicaraguan resistance ceased on February 29. Unlike 1986, there would be no second vote for the administration. The Speaker locked the door on all further legislative action until the rebels and the government reached a cease-fire agreement.

The deadlock in Washington was a boon to the Sandinistas, who acted swiftly to reap advantages. On February 18, Cardinal Obando, the mutually accepted mediator, had advanced a 30-day cease-fire proposal based on four points within the framework of the Esquipulas II accords:

- General amnesty
- Restoration of civil liberties
- Dialogue with the internal opposition
- Rescinding of the draft law.

The democratic bias in the Cardinal's proposal was hailed by the contras, but alarmed the Sandinistas. They did not wish to spoil the Speaker's hand just before the March 3 vote, and thus they delayed any action on its terms. But the week after the vote, Ortega fired the Cardinal as mediator and announced that the FSLN would talk directly with the contras at Sapoa, a town on the border between Costa Rica and Nicaragua. At the same time, the Sandinista Army launched an offensive into the Bocay valley region. The vanguard of the offensive was a foray of several thousand troops into Honduras to capture the Contras' Strategic Command. Movement of gasoline depots and reserve units suggest the assault was planned a month in advance, or at the same time Ortega made the concessions that kept the Arias peace plan alive and scuttled the administration's policy. On March 15, President Reagan sent 3,000 U.S. troops to Honduras in a move widely criticized by the Left.

The contras had escaped destruction, but remained in a dire predicament. According to Calero, "We had to do something. There were 5,000 men trapped in the Bocay, with only two or three days of food. There was no way we could accommodate them in Honduras, because our possibilities of credit were exhausted there—we were still paying the debt of 1985. I thought Sapoa was our only hope."[15]

This was the consensus of the resistance leadership. The long-awaited encounter between contras and Sandinistas thus took place on March 23. Daniel and Humberto Ortega headed the FSLN delegation. The resistance was represented by Calero, Cesar, and Sanchez (who acted, informally, as Bermudez's deputy).

The meeting produced an agreement for a 60-day truce to determine, among other things:

- Seven cease-fire enclaves, into which the rebels would move by April 15
- "Unrestricted freedom of expression" in Nicaragua (the only specific political commitment in the Sapoa agreement)
- Delivery of humanitarian aid in the enclaves by a neutral organization
- Resistance representatives to participate in a national dialogue to negotiate democratic reform
- A Verification Commission to monitor compliance

- High-level negotiations in Managua for a "definitive ceasefire."[16]

The immediate price for the agreement had been that the rebels drop their conditions to holding the talks for a definitive cease-fire. The agenda of reform was thus left hostage to a promise for future discussion.

§§   How the rebels undermined their own weak position still further through foolish internal strife

The immediate benefit to the resistance of the Sapoa agreement was a $17.7 million U.S. humanitarian aid package, passed on March 31. According to Donald Castillo, the secretary for international relations of the resistance, "Almost everybody agreed that this first agreement was not so bad for us. We would not have to disarm at once, the Sandinistas made certain political concessions, and it was envisioned that the enclaves would provide over 20,000 square kilometers of territory."[17]

But internal factors caused the resistance position to wilt rapidly in later talks. The Sandinistas' most devastating weapon was ambiguity. They marked the contras' nervousness and lost no chance to inflame it. According to Rene Herrera, a rebel negotiator at the Technical-Level Talks that followed Sapoa, the FSLN's first proposals were specific and not unfavorable to the resistance. In successive rounds they became steadily more vague and more negative, particularly on the vital matter of the enclaves. As Calero lamented,

> Lack of dexterity on the part of our technical commission was perhaps a problem. But this was an unmistakable opportunity to expose the intransigence of the Sandinistas. My opinion was that these were tough decisions, and somebody had to take them. Because of subsequent misgivings, we lost out. Sanchez signed on,

but later was sorry. Cesar wouldn't defend [the Sapoa agreement], and stayed quietly in Costa Rica. I wanted Bermudez to be there, but he said he would agree to anything as long as what the Cardinal had said was in it.[18]

Pressure to reach an agreement with the Sandinistas before the end of the truce on May 30 thickened the volatile atmosphere in the resistance leadership. Indeed, for the contras, the Sapoa truce was turning into a time bomb with a 60-day fuse.

Bermudez had endorsed the Sapoa accord; now he publicly expressed reservations. Apart from the substantive problems, other concerns were at work. He had feared that Calero would try to isolate him by appealing to the combatants over his head or by striking a deal with Cesar as he had attempted to do in 1985. Indeed, Sapoa itself had been the product of a convergence between Cesar and Calero. To forestall such a possibility and exert some control over the talks' content, Bermudez had followed a strategy of rotating the members of the combatant delegation. Worried by terms negotiated in the technical round, Bermudez attempted to restrain the rebel delegation from further concessions. This he did by banning the combatants' representatives from the first round of cease-fire talks—Managua I—scheduled for April 15. Thus "Toño" and "Rigoberto," as well as Aristides Sanchez, were not allowed to attend. The willingness or ability of the resistance to negotiate a definitive cease-fire was now in doubt.

Cesar saw the advantages of neutrality in what was becoming a duel-to-the-death between Calero and Bermudez. A victory by Calero, reducing Bermudez, would complete Cesar's own isolation. But Bermudez in the long term was helpless without a civilian ally. Cesar was ideal for such a role. His realignment took place in the fortnight after the technical talks. Cesar agreed with Calero (as did all of the directorate except Sanchez, who supported Bermudez) that sufficient progress had been made to warrant a new round

of talks with the Sandinistas in Managua from April 15 to
18. But Calero also began to shorten the distance between
himself and Bermudez.

Sensing the opportunity to make political capital out of
this schism, the Sandinistas took back concessions made at
the technical round. The signing of an enclave agreement
had been a condition of U.S. aid; to begin with, the Sandinistas had to promise not to shoot at the supply vehicles.
Once the contras moved into the cease-fire zones, aid would
flow.

The Sandinistas now pointed to Bermudez, arguing
that the contras were interested in the cease-fire talks only
to buy time to refurbish their troops. Rather than agreeing
on a political agenda, the government proposed that the
resistance retreat to their zones and lay down arms by July
1. Democratization would then be the subject of future
talks. "'Managua I' led nowhere," says Calero. "All that we
got was the chance to come back to Managua."[19]

From April 28 to 30, Calero led a second round of
talks—Managua II—at which the Sandinistas hardened
their position. They attached the question of supply to the
agreement on a definitive *in situ* (as opposed to an enclave-
based) cease-fire. Not only would this have worsened the
highly vulnerable position of the northern front combatants; it also would have allowed the Sandinistas to evade
the obligations of amnesty, and resistance participation
in the national dialogue, which would have been triggered
by the enclave agreement. The resistance rejected this
proposal.

Managua I and II were shrewd, crippling blows. By
linking the matter of resupply to an impossible agreement
on the cease-fire, the FSLN gave the contras three stark
choices: surrender, starve, or retreat. During a two week
period more than 5,000 troops poured back into Honduras,
flooding the area around Yamales, the principal contra
camp. The rapidly collapsing northern front now posed an
extreme test of the leadership's ability to provide for rebel
units and civilian refugees alike. Half the 60-day truce had

elapsed without agreement on a cease-fire or procedures for resupply.

The FSLN presented conditions that were unacceptable to all members of the resistance. The talks themselves then became an issue. Clearly, nothing could be obtained as long as the resistance remained divided. According to Calero, "After that, we decided not to return to Managua for further talks."

§§ How the confusion led to a mutiny in the rebel ranks

No episode better illustrates the complexity of the forces that shape the Nicaraguan Resistance—interest, idealism, kinship, irrationality, ambition, history, and, above all, chance—than the dissidence that followed the deadlock in the talks.

The vacuum in Washington had precipitated a vacuum in the resistance. According to Donald Castillo, "Nobody knew where anyone was standing—neither Calero, nor Cesar, nor Bermudez, nor the troops."[20] The level of mistrust was extremely high. A rumor that Calero had struck a secret deal during a private encounter with Humberto Ortega spread like wildfire. Supposedly he was guaranteed the leadership of the internal opposition if he quit the contras. The Somoza dynasty had ruled Nicaragua for 40 years through such subversive tactics.

Sapoa was not the cause of the revolt, but it provided the conditions for a challenge to the institutional balance of the resistance. Bosco Matamoros complained that

> the United States failed to provide support after Sapoa for us to overcome the confusion that arose in the troops. What emerged from Sapoa was a growing anarchy that threatened not only the institutionality of the Directorate, but the very existence of the Resistance. Instead of a hundred flowers, a hundred cactuses bloomed.[21]

It was such confusion that prompted a number of field commanders, including some who had been part of the resistance negotiating commission, to question Bermudez's right to ban representatives of the combatants from the talks. Calero pounced on this opportunity to reclaim his mastery over the military and civilian wings of the movement. Moving actively, if obscurely, against Bermudez, he encouraged the dissidents to sharpen their grievances. On May 2, the popular regional commanders "Toño," "Rigoberto," and "Fernando" published a petition urging his ouster. Half of the 30-odd field commanders of the resistance signed on, including some of the most valuable and well liked. Key civilian associates of Calero also supported the petition, led by Morales Carazo, and Enrique Sanchez ("Cuco"), the brother of Aristides. The petition revived the charges of the field commanders' 1984 grievance, accusing Bermudez of tolerating corruption, poor leadership, and a dictatorial style.

Bermudez responded by accusing Calero of reckless disloyalty and hinted that he too could uncover proofs of malfeasance. Denouncing the invisible hand behind the revolt, he snapped, "Whoever that might have been, he was very stupid. Didn't he realize I have a high percentage of support in this organization? Even if it isn't 100 per cent, it is enough to destroy the organization."[22]

Relations between Bermudez and Calero frayed visibly, as each appealed to the directorate to hamstring the other. Calero counted on Chamorro and Ferrey; Bermudez on Sanchez only. Alfredo Cesar, who had hoped to steer a neutral course, saw plainly that the removal of Bermudez would make him Calero's next target. In perhaps the oddest of the rebels' odd alliances, he embraced Bermudez, the hard-line commander and proposed that Bermudez join the negotiating commission, a move Calero roundly opposed.

The truth is that Bermudez's position was in deadly jeopardy and probably could not have been rescued except from outside. The obscure axis in the resistance power structure suddenly emerged with dazzling force to save him. In a *coup de main* that was advised by the CIA, requested by Bermudez, and enforced by the Honduran military, "Toño" and "Rigoberto" were arrested on May 4 in the midst of a press conference and deported to Miami.

This move seemed to restore order, if not unity. According to Alfredo Cesar, at this stage the directors' differences were "on ice." Bermudez and the directorate had arrived in Washington to consult with administration officials. The centerpiece of the visit, a session with Secretary of State Shultz, underscored the importance of unity. But the State Department seems to have been ignorant of the depth of the rift between the directors. They themselves misjudged the forces that were bubbling beneath them.

Chance events suddenly caused the dissidence to erupt into full-fledged mutiny. The schism ceased to concern the issue of negotiations and degenerated into a naked struggle for power. One of the commanders marked by Bermudez for arrest, "Fernando," had eluded capture and absconded to the camp at Yamales. Twenty-nine-year-old "Fernando" was a popular leader of *campesino* stock who had prepared for an evangelical ministry before joining the contras. Along with "Rigoberto," he had helped command the resistance's 7,000-man push against the mining region in December. On December 9, he claimed the allegiance of between 2,000 and 3,000 combatants garrisoned at Yamales and disowned the authority of the Strategic Command, pending Bermudez's dismissal. Bermudez hastily flew back from a meeting in Miami to placate "Fernando."

Calero at once moved to fire Bermudez, disregarding the injunctions of the administration. On May 9, Calero, Ferrey, and Chamorro formally sought Bermudez's dismissal. Four votes out of the five-member directorate were needed to remove Bermudez. He was saved when Cesar joined Sanchez to oppose a vote.

Chamorro and Ferrey were then sent to Honduras to arrange a compromise, in which the Commanders' Council, including Bermudez and the dissident commanders, would meet with the directorate to settle their differences. Hopes of reconciling the dissidents with Bermudez diminished the next day, when two men sent out by "Fernando" for supplies were killed in a fracas with Bermudez loyalists. Deeply dismayed, "Fernando" was lured out of Yamales by Honduran, U.S., and resistance officials on the pretext of talks to reduce the tension, and then he was arrested.

This decisive stroke severed the leaders of the mutiny from their troops; it was still necessary to keep the situation from deteriorating into anarchy. The camp remained in the hands of junior officers, who were "much less understanding, politically, and also somewhat less responsible," according to one of the resistance directors, who adds, "it was a very, very dangerous situation."[23] They threatened to take Bermudez hostage if he approached the camp.

Bermudez had saved his position, but his power was still in doubt. Some of the dissidents were willing to accept his authority, but on the condition that members of his Strategic Command, such as "Mike Lima," "El Quiche," and "Mack" be removed. The Strategic Command now became the issue. A majority vote of the directorate could still force Bermudez to accept the compromise meeting, which would impose a new general staff on him.

Chamorro says that U.S. officials told him the Hondurans supported Bermudez unconditionally and wanted to deport "Fernando" immediately. Nevertheless, on May 10, Chamorro met with a delegation of five Honduran colonels at Ojo de Agua, who agreed not to expel "Fernando" and to permit the compromise meeting between the council, Bermudez, and the directorate to take place in Honduras.

The next day, at a meeting attended by U.S. and Honduran officials, Bermudez informed Chamorro he would never talk with a "bunch of mutineers," or submit to being judged by a "court hauled in from the outside." He insisted that the dissidence was a military matter under the jurisdiction of the military authorities. Chamorro charged Bermudez with insubordination.

> We had an argument over the voluntary character of the Resistance army. I said this was a clear case of

disobedience of the civilian authority of the Directorate. The strategic command must obey orders, not
make them; the civilian power must give orders, not
take them. To the astonishment both of the Americans
and of Bermudez, the Honduran colonels concurred:
they said that it should be the civilian Directorate
which settled the case of the dissidents. Bermudez
turned very pale.[24]

Chamorro then left for Miami to set up the compromise
meeting. But in the meantime the CIA had pressed the
Hondurans, who reversed their decision. The Hondurans
had undertaken no formal commitment to support Chamorro's proposal and in any case took a dim view of the
growing anarchy on their territory. As one journalist noted,
"The dissidents were driving them up the wall with their
press conferences."[25] "Fernando" was politely deported to
Miami.

The deportation was the last straw for Chamorro. Inspired by Calero, he determined that he could no longer
remain in the same movement as Bermudez. In an acrid
meeting of the directorate, held in Miami on May 14, he
demanded the chief commander's ouster.

On the face of it, Bermudez's unilateral fiats warranted
his dismissal; but, at the time, such a course ran a high risk
of shattering the resistance. The pragmatic Sanchez clearly
saw the risk to the resistance as well as the threat to his
own position. Says Sanchez:

What happened was this: the people under Calero who
controlled the finances in Honduras mounted this
thing; they took advantage of the negotiations, a
delicate moment, in order to foster the rebellion, as a
way to reduce Bermudez. That way they would end up
with their own people in finance, and with these kids
in the military. Things were completely out of control.
It was necessary to preserve the institutionality of the
Resistance.[26]

On the pretext of making a photocopy of Chamorro's proposal, Sanchez left the room and telephoned the CIA in Washington.

"Big George," the CIA officer in charge, requested that his call be placed over a speaker and launched a diatribe against Chamorro, calling him an "imbecile." He warned that if Bermudez were fired, the United States would never again give a penny to the resistance. According to Calero, "That was humiliating. Completely out of bounds. I rejected it."[27] But in fact this shocking intervention broke the last opposition to Bermudez. Calero now looked almost as isolated from Honduras as Cruz had been in 1986. His civilian and military allies were banished to Miami. The Americans no longer trusted him. The deportation of "Fernando" had beheaded the leadership of the dissident troops. The rebels themselves, confused and angry, remained sullenly neutral in the camps.

While all this was happening, the Sandinistas launched a diplomatic initiative, taking advantage of the contras' impotence. Assistant Foreign Minister Victor Hugo Tinoco arrived in Miami from Nicaragua with a new proposal for talks in Managua from May 25 to 28, two days before the Sapoa truce expired.

The directorate at once issued a communiqué announcing that it had "closed the case" and turned its attention to the impending round of continuing talks in Managua. On May 23, it was announced that Bermudez would join the negotiating committee. Calero's absence from the team underscored the low ebb of his political fortunes.

Who sinned against the institutionality of the resistance? The demand of the field commanders for a greater stake in the strategic decision-making process was long-standing and legitimate. Indeed, this is what lends poignancy to their failure. The proper vehicle for their claim was the Commanders' Council. When this was unjustly suppressed, they sought to raise the dispute as a political matter germane to the directorate. When Bermudez defied Chamorro, there was, in principle, good cause to censure the chief commander.

It is far more difficult to say who *upheld* the institutionality of the resistance. From the moment Chamorro elevated this quarrel to the directorate, the dispute became a struggle for mastery of the movement. If Chamorro were to have his way, the combined political and military powers would again have been deposited with Calero. Bermudez fought to save his own skin and, by extension, that of the independent directors. So did Sanchez, who perceived the dispute as a threat to the political and personal balance of the resistance leadership. What had resurfaced here—in the shape of a duel between Bermudez and Calero—was the eternal conflict between unity and equilibrium and between people and power in the resistance. Sanchez and Chamorro thrashed out the matter: one upheld the principle, the other the practice behind the institution of a united rebel force under a balanced, civilian leadership.

Although matters were very murky, Chamorro did not perceive what was going on as well as others. Egged on by Calero, he had fastened on to a very noble standard and charged, heedless as a knight, into the melee. Throughout Nicaragua's history, this ancestral Chamorro trait has sometimes led to great feats. This time it secured only the young scion's untimely political death and unkind perpetuation in the contras of his sobriquet "Pedro el Bruto" (Peter the Dunce).

In the final analysis, the old vice of Nicaraguan politics reaffirmed itself. An external power had to be summoned, like a genie, to recast the order that the Nicaraguans themselves had marred. By this intervention, the contras' nationalist character was again besmirched and with it, their legitimacy. Institutionality was saved but at incalculable cost to credibility.

§§   How the mutiny led to great demoralization among the contras

Without doubt, the contras were gravely weakened by this schism. This time the resistance lost face in the eyes of not only the world but its own members and closest friends.

The human cost of the revolt cannot be understated. The combatants sickened at the thought that they had been manipulated for the sake of personal power struggles.

Many people doubted whether the combatants' cynicism toward the civilian leadership could be overcome. Indeed, some rebels abandoned the struggle. Large numbers of ex-contras undertook the journey by foot to the United States: one group found its way to Miami, another was detained in Brownsville, Texas. "Fernando" is now working at a shoe factory in Miami. The case of 34-year-old "Rigoberto" had to impress the rank and file. A widely respected small farmer, he had collaborated with the Sandinistas against Somoza, and in the contra ranks rose naturally to lead one of the principal regional commands, the Jorge Salazar I. After his deportation to Miami, his family's ration in the refugee settlement was cut; his wife and children were forced to flee back to an uncertain fate in Nicaragua.

"Rigoberto" wrote bitterly to the combatants:

> You can see now that our leaders never had the faintest intention of winning this war, and that they never intended to return to Nicaragua . . . while the Sandinistas built their armies and prepared their cadres for military and political challenges, our cadres were trained simply to put up with hunger. . . .
>
> Now some of us are opening our eyes, and we see that . . . we were being used for personal interests by some, and as a tool for "containment" by others: for seven years we were used. . . .
>
> Many of you will ask, why we had not done so before, and I will tell you that unfortunately because of love for our cause and for the sake of unity we became accomplices to our own ills. . . . You are the witnesses of this, for you have lived it with your own flesh.[28]

Yet the intrinsic strength of the cause asserted itself. It is indeed remarkable that many who joined the resistance have left it, but, like Cruz, few have recanted their aims.

"Rigoberto" urged the combatants to maintain their unity and to work for purifying the resistance for only the Sandinistas would gain by their dispersal. The dissidents requested a return to their commands; when they were rebuffed, they appealed to President Reagan in a letter of September 1988:

> We want to continue our fight to the end, come what may. We understand completely that the question of further assistance is difficult at best, but we want to go on as long as possible. If we lose, we want to lose with our dignity intact, as honest men who have failed in an honest cause. From our viewpoint, the immediate and more serious problem is not the lack of material assistance—we all fought for one and a half years in Nicaragua during the 1984–85 cutoff—but the growing demoralization of the combatants that is rooted in this unresolved crisis. We want to stop the outflow of fighters, most of them making their way illegally to the United States, who have chosen to abandon the fight rather than endure the arrogance, the continuing corruption, the intimidation and threats against everyone who is seen as a "sympathizer" of the dissident movement.[29]

One cannot help but see that the recurring theme of the contras' story is the failure of their leadership. Hindsight may well concur that this was the moment for a true leader to sever his people's connection with a vacillating, sanctimonious ally and to carry on the struggle. The history of many republics begins with such an act, against all odds. But no such leader emerged. Who had been rendered conspicuous by strength and honesty? Who had shown courage and wisdom? Who had shown he could be trusted with power? Who had shown a truly national calling?

No one, is the sad answer. Perhaps these directors faced circumstances that no one could overcome without mishap. But many of the contras' most appalling plights were of their own making. This mutiny need never have happened:

had Calero not been so untrustworthy, Sanchez so cynical, Cesar so misleading, Chamorro so guileless, and Bermudez so insecure, and had the combatants benefited from the political education that their leaders denied them for so long. In spite of the bravery and honesty of individuals, can anyone wonder that the Nicaraguan resistance had such an ignominious career?

§§   How the Sandinistas' disregard of the Arias plan led to a new effort at bipartisanship, which failed because of the U.S. election campaign

As mid-1988 approached, the irony in Rep. Slattery's words of February—"You'll be feeding the people in the cease-fire zones. They will flock to you there"—became complete. Not only had there been no agreement on the zones; the deteriorating situation in Nicaragua spawned a new exodus. Costa Rican public health officials estimate that between 1,000 and 2,000 refugees a month were illegally crossing the border. In Honduras, the U.S. Agency for International Development (AID) was soon feeding over 12,000 contras and 45,000 dependents.

The Sandinistas harshened their terms. Rather than seeking a compromise, they sought to squeeze the most out of their improved circumstances. They dismissed as outlandish a calendar advanced by the resistance of specific steps for democratization within the framework of Esquipulas. Instead, they proposed adhering to general guidelines to be worked out in further dialogue. When the rebels dismissed this offer, the FSLN refused to allow resupply operations. Talks broke down on June 9, never, it seemed, to resume.

Things fared badly for the internal opposition as well. Daily the wires spoke of appalling events. A hunger strike by union workers met with brutal coercion by state security. Interior Minister Borge summoned a radio newscaster,

José Castillo, to his office and socked him in the mouth. On July 10, an important opposition rally at Nandaime was broken up, not by the "divine mobs" (or *turbas*) as ordinarily happened, but by government forces, indicating official concern to keep dissent in hand. Thirty-eight democratic leaders were jailed. The FSLN accused the CIA of orchestrating the rally and subsequent riot and expelled the U.S. ambassador.

Speaker Wright had warned that neither side should use the truce as an opportunity to strengthen its position. But the contras' plight continued to worsen. No enclave agreement had been reached, and the FSLN refused to allow food and medical shipments. Despite Sandinista protests that this violated the spirit of the Sapoa accords, Wright approved an administration plan to supply the rebels with cash payments in cordobas. In a bizarre experiment, hundreds of Tennessee mules were airlifted to Honduras to carry relief bundles to the beleaguered contras in Nicaragua.

Embarrassed by the turn of events, interest renewed in Congress to craft a new bipartisan initiative. The new proposal came from the Senate, in talks between Minority Leader Dole and Majority Leader Byrd. But, as so often happened, domestic political events—the U.S. presidential elections—intruded to thwart a compromise.

Dole was angling for the vice-presidential nomination. If he could broker a contra deal that healed the rift between Democrats and Republicans, he would strengthen his hand. The Republicans wanted mainly to shore up the contras so they could move into the cease-fire zones. But their package was presented to the Democrats on the night before recess for the Democratic Convention. As one Senate staffer observed, "the Democrats thought it was a trick. Though Dole swore it wasn't, no one would sign on, especially after Bentsen [a firm contra supporter] was nominated."

Embarrassed at the divisions in their own party, the Democrats circled wagons around the status quo. They advanced a counterproposal, which contained only humanitarian aid and laid stringent conditions for a second vote. The talks between Democrats and Republicans bogged down. According to a Republican participant, Dole, with the support of Alfredo Cesar, was eager to press the compromise for political reasons,

> but everyone from Helms to Kassebaum refused to sign on. On Monday, Dole held a meeting in his office, to tell us we had no choice but to accept. It was incredible: his desk at one end, and the chairs set up in rows, as if for a lecture, in front of it. [NSC adviser] Powell stood beside him. Powell was obviously hedging, and uncomfortable with the package, but said he could live with it. Then Senator McCain spoke against it for five minutes, and everybody refused to sign. Powell breathed a sigh of relief. Dole was furious, and wouldn't return our calls for about a week after that. He had to go to Byrd and say, "I'm sorry, it didn't come through." Byrd was livid too. He blamed a "small band of conservatives" for torpedoing the deal, even though we were all against it.[30]

Dole was forced to criticize all the things he had lobbied for previously. The Senate compromise broke down, as Democrats and Republicans voted for their respective packages along strict party lines. The failure of the bipartisan proposal, amidst recriminations, badly burned Alfredo Cesar both in Congress and in the resistance. Although he had assured both sides of his support, he seemed unable to get results from anybody.

§§   The resistance adrift

In July, the Assembly of the resistance met in the Dominican Republic for a tumultuous session. Bribery, intimidation, and denial of access to the meeting room were widely reported. A new directorate emerged, one of distinctively lower caliber than the old and reflecting the loss of prestige of the resistance. Bermudez, in what appears to have been a defensive move, was installed as a director, with 44 votes. Calero and Cesar remained, with about 30 votes each. Chamorro was ousted and replaced by Wilfredo Montalvan, an obscure political hack. Ferrey left of her own will. Robelo, who had slipped out of the resistance early in the year, was not missed.

Options outside the armed resistance were beginning to look more attractive for Cesar, as they had for Robelo. In September, he explored the possibility of stepping down from the directorate. For such a move to be effective, he would have to maintain the support of the moderate congressmen. As he explained on August 11, "The key groups he and his supporters were trying to influence and work with included: the more hardline faction in the resistance, the Central American Presidents (specifically Arias and Cerezo), and the 'swing' Democrats in Congress, represented by Spratt, McCurdy, Carper, and Slattery."[31] The February 3 vote had undermined him, since his 1987 alliance with Bermudez and Calero had been based on the premise that the two-track approach, which stressed the diplomatic and political as well as military aspects of the struggle, would win the support of Congress.

The worsening plight of Nicaragua had not rewritten Cesar's political map. As he explained to the congressmen,

> Recent political developments in Central America further undercut the moderates in the Resistance. Secretary of State Shultz visited the region on two separate occasions recently. His inability to get the Guatemalan or Costa Rican Presidents to come down hard on the Sandinistas after the events of July 10 in Managua [the reference is to Nandaime—Ed.], simply reinforced the perception among hardliners that the political/diplomatic track had little to offer them. . . . [32]

Cesar said also that he wished to make his resignation "in a very correct manner," without recriminations against his colleagues on the directorate or recanting his aims in the armed resistance. He wished to "confront the 'swing' Democrats and the Central American presidents with the consequences of their decisions. Unwilling to support a genuine middle course . . . they will now have to deal with the hardliners in the Resistance and more importantly, with a Sandinista government no longer facing any military pressure. . . . "[33] These cautious moves suggest he was poising himself, like Robelo, to be the key link between armed resistance and internal opposition in a future political strategy.

At length Cesar decided to stay in the resistance. No great advantage was to be derived from leaving. It seems also as if he were anticipating events in Venezuela, where his Social-Democratic ally, Carlos Andres Perez, was the likely winner of reelection to the presidency. One must also report that a rumor circulated to the effect that his exploration of a return to Nicaragua met with a cold shoulder from the internal opposition and Sandinistas alike.

If Cesar thought his own position in the leadership was weak, he had only to look around him for consolation. Calero was virtually a pariah. Bermudez felt awkward in his newly prominent seat and was persuaded of the wisdom of keeping Cesar by his side, lest Calero profit by blaming him for driving yet another liberal from the contra leadership.

The contras observed that they seemed to have been doing as poorly without an enclave agreement as they expected to do with one and thus sought to renew negotiations with the Sandinistas. They abandoned the preconditions for talks, such as the calendar advanced in June. In September, Bermudez, Sanchez, and Cesar met with Speaker Wright to secure bipartisan support for this move. But Wright remained noncommittal, allowing only that the leadership would endorse whatever agreement the contras first worked out with the Sandinistas. What little practical results emerged from this meeting were drowned in the outcry over the Speaker's ill-advised remarks on CIA participation at the Nandaime rally. The Sandinistas remained inflexible.

§§ The end of an era

The contras were now adrift, pending the U.S. elections. The upswing of George Bush's fortunes revived hopes that the last had not been heard of the two-track policy in Nicaragua, though no one expected him to show the same commitment to the rebel cause as had Reagan. Negotiations and the military track alike were put on hold as Congress and Central America awaited the next administration.

The contra leadership entered a period of political irrelevance. Its concerns, at this point, were largely administrative and self-centered. In October, the directors attempted to fire Somarriba as financial comptroller in an effort to gain greater independence with the Nicaraguan Resistance fund. This move was resisted by the United States. "The CIA said they would appoint an American auditor to account for every piece of chewing gum they bought," said one official charged with implementing the policy, "and that was the end of that."[34]

Questions even began to arise about the need for a political leadership in the resistance. As one disaffected rebel official wrote in November:

> The ideal for which we fought is not the driving force of the resistance today. . . . Totally absurd and unreal ambitions have made the leadership of the Resistance the final purpose of the politicians. The summit of power. In other words, to be a Director of the Resistance is the non-plus-ultra of the exiled politician. The true purpose of the Resistance has been lost. It has become a government in exile to govern, not the exiled, nor the Nicaraguans, but itself.[35]

The election of George Bush, together with a reaffirmed Democratic mandate in both Houses, suggested that the principal priority of the new administration would be domestic—to rebuild a bipartisan consensus even at the expense of short-term interests in Central America. The contras made tentative contacts with the new administration through Bush adviser William Perry, a former aide to Senate Foreign Relations Committee Chairman Richard Lugar. "I don't know of anyone on the team who wants to abandon the Contras," said Perry, "but as a practical matter, there just isn't going to be a vote on this in the near future, and no one wants to start off with a confrontation. Rhetoric is going to have to square up with reality."[36]

Almost unnoticed, the Reagan administration uttered its last on Nicaragua. Shortly after Bush's victory, it announced it would not request further military aid for the contras.

Postscript

§§ After Reagan: how the search for an "ideal resistance" came to an end

§§ After Reagan: how the search for an "ideal resistance" came to an end

By 1989 the contras were little more than spectators of their own fate.

James A. Baker, the new secretary of state, announced in February that Bernard W. Aronson, a former Democratic labor lobbyist, would replace Elliott Abrams. A glimpse of Aronson's views can be found in the October 1988 proposal from Freedom House, a bipartisan group that mustered the support of moderates and centrists for the two-track policy. It reflected the common wisdom of the times: the initiative must be recaptured for democracy in Central America; the Arias plan is the least unattractive alternative; a calendar of compliance must be reattached to the plan. Freedom House revived the Costa Rican president's warning that all sides would be free to do as they thought fit if the agreement failed:

> The Esquipulas II accords ... with their commitment to securing peace through the establishment of full democratic freedom in all countries of the region ... still offer the soundest basis for an effort to rebuild an

125

effective and bi-partisan US policy in Central America. We urge the new Administration and the new Congress to join together to marshal all our political and diplomatic resources . . . for a new and more rigorous test of the Esquipulas agreement during the first months of the new term."[1]

The Sandinistas' international configuration needed rethinking too, particularly with respect to the old Contadora bloc. Panama and El Salvador displaced Nicaragua as the principal focus of U.S. concern. Elections in Mexico and Venezuela brought to power deeply troubled coalitions with a strong interest in pursuing pragmatic policies, as well as improving relations with the United States. The return to the Venezuelan presidency of Cesar's ally, Carlos Andres Perez, promised to sustain, if not to stiffen, the diplomatic pressure for reform in Nicaragua. Presidential elections in El Salvador, Honduras, and Costa Rica showed signs of a conservative turn in 1989, dissipating what little urge might have remained in those countries to give the Sandinistas the benefit of the doubt on any matter. The erosion of Soviet prestige loomed large in the backdrop, though neither the USSR nor its proxies showed concrete signs of reducing their investment in the region.

On February 14, the Arias plan was once again raised from the grave by last-minute concessions from the Sandinistas. Ortega bought time: one year, in exchange for a promise to grant elections in February 1990. Now, as Arias had intended, the struggle was removed to the political arena. By fits and starts, the internal opposition tortuously set aside its differences to line up behind the candidacy of Violeta Chamorro. As might be expected, contradictory signs came from the resistance.

The prevailing strain recognized the need to roll with the changes. As an internal strategy paper put it, 1989 promised "to be the year of diplomacy."[2] Voluntary restraint would be called for in the military arm and a renewed effort at building bridges with the internal opposition. Rather than attempting to even the odds by shoring up the resistance with military aid, the contras would call on the United States and allies to undercut the FSLN by diplomacy, chiseling at its ties to Cuba and the USSR. The contras would lay down their arms, they said, if the elections were free and fair.

Great skepticism attended the question of whether the contras could sustain the unity needed for such a long-term approach. Nevertheless, this strategy suggested a sober assessment of practical possibilities. The same calculation that kept the Arias plan alive could now work in favor of the rebels: until after the elections, who would dare take the responsibility for burying them?

In late March 1989, the Bush administration reached an agreement with the Democrats to continue supplying "humanitarian" aid to the contras until the Nicaraguan elections 11 months later. During that period, a ponderous international supervision was mobilized for the elections from all quarters of the free world. The centerpiece of the effort, a blue-helmeted UN peacekeeping force, opaqued the U.S. rationale for supporting a political/military guarantee such as the Nicaraguan Resistance. Indeed, beyond the purposes of decorum, it soon became apparent that the contras no longer were an instrument of policy. If anything, the new administration seemed to perceive them as an obstacle in the way of a new policy. Thus closed the Americans' search for the "ideal resistance" that is the subject of this book. For all purposes, the contras were again left to their own devices.

With no better prospects, the rank-and-file hunkered down in their camps in Honduras and Nicaragua, self-appointed guarantors of the purity of the electoral process. Their political leaders split: some to exile and well-deserved obscurity in Miami, some to sit and wait in Honduras, some to the rugged campaign with Violeta Chamorro in Nicaragua. The elections were watched avidly, if skeptically, by all; they afforded the rare hope of creating a new community of interest among Nicaraguans. That in turn encouraged waiting, the slow unfolding of diplomacy, and the painstaking assembly of coalitions—rather than a renewed call to arms. And in bloody El Salvador and Guatemala, the same attenuating forces were at work.

§§   The balance: what the contras achieved and the true nature of their failure

The contras' moment had passed. But time no longer smiled on the Sandinistas. Their feverish visions of conquest and permanent revolution now merely aggravated an internal fit over how to pay the bills for the food, shelter, and comforts they had promised. Daniel Ortega's simple slogan, "All Will Be Better," was the oracle of his own defeat. Revolution demands sacrifice; the FSLN dared ask nothing more of the Nicaraguan people. The Marxist-Leninist wave that in 1980 seemed poised to tinge the map of all the isthmus had crested. This is what the contras achieved. In the last years of the cold war, when time was a most precious commodity, they bought time for Nicaragua's neighboring republics—curiously, the vague original goal of the Reagan contra policy. The moment of revolution, too, had passed.

In what concrete sense did the contras fail? The Sandinistas' radical expedients in 1987 and 1988 show beyond doubt that the resistance was palpably close to some sort of military success. Had the narrow vote of February 3 gone the other way, it is highly possible the contras could have forced a stalemate. For the Sandinistas, that could well have meant an explosion, rather than the quicksand in which the promise of elections had mired them.

Bad luck accounts for the military debacle, yet much of the contras' bad luck was of their own making. The debacle was but the mere effect and circumstantial fringe of the contras' real failing. A more penetrating judgment must consider that the contras' commission was not simply to whip the Sandinistas and save El Salvador in the bargain, as their U.S. backers yearned: it was to transcend Nicaragua's past, to correct the political vices arising from a tradition of irresponsibility at every juncture of society.

This called for one thing: a leadership compelled to answer to its followers. Democracy has no monopoly on this principle. But, through the republican device of regular alternation of power, it starts from the principle of power as a trust for the people.

All democracies emerge from a past that does not bear looking into. With greater or lesser momentum, the peoples' energies and the ambitions of their chiefs are coaxed into institutions that preserve power as a trust for the commonweal. But long before that, the compulsion to answer to the public trust must ripen as a rich private inspiration in the leading citizenry. Even that is rarely sufficient for democracy to flourish. Those private convictions must be coupled with uncommon public ability.

This is where the contras went astray. Especially after 1987, the administration spared no effort of nurture for democratic forms in the resistance. Assemblies, committees, secretariats came and went; declarations, charters, covenants solemnly succeeded one another. But the main fault ran through individuals, not institutions. As the old proverb says, *"Quod natura non dat, Salamanca non facet."* The Americans could not put in what the Nicaraguans did not have.

This is therefore above all a study in the failure of leadership. In the final reckoning, the leaders in the resistance fell short of the noble ideals they presumed to embody. Character, strength, vision, prestige—the specific faults of specific leaders have already been scrutinized. The men at the top were well aware of their own shortcomings. Rather than open themselves to criticism and improvement, they shielded themselves behind myths of indispensability and dodged any true accounting.

Would things have gone better if the resistance had been led by better men? The extraordinary attention commanded by the career of the hapless Arturo Cruz shows that the answer is almost certainly yes. But an unnatural process of selection—of which Cruz's elevation is itself the prime example—worsened the problem of leadership. The Americans, in Congress and the administration alike, could not help but tilt the career ladder in the resistance toward meeting their own political and bureaucratic regards; the Nicaraguans could not help but take advantage of this.

Such temporizing virtually guaranteed that the movement would be presided by malleable men: political tacticians, not democratic statesmen. Alfredo Cesar, who crashed the gates through bold Machiavellian strokes, was the exception that proved the rule. It is easy to see why he never earned anyone's trust. In due course, those with power conspired among themselves to preempt the natural rise of talent from the ranks. Idealism was frustrated; ambition warped; integrity ridiculed; courage wasted. The pathetic calls of the regional commanders for political education for their men, so long evaded, are one glaring example. The onus of this judgment rests with Bermudez and Calero.

It was such mingy calculating that left the contras' leadership open to devastating charges of incompetence and duplicity. They seemed to grudge, not embrace, democracy. Amends were marred by such frequent signs of bad faith that progress was constantly swallowed in recriminations. In the end, it all added up to a crisis of credibility.

The resistance never made clear that it could ever be held to account by anyone more than its strategic patrons. At a vital juncture, a few congressmen's doubts that the administration could be trusted for this purpose failed to be overcome, and the tables were turned. Such was the significance of the razor-thin vote on February 3, such the fallout of the Iran-Contra scandal. As with Belshazzar in the fable of the feast, the policy was weighed and weighed in the balance, and found wanting. By this vote the contras' fate was certainly hastened. But had it not been sealed long before that, and by their own deeds?

Thus it is necessary to cast things into perspective by

qualifying what is written above. The success and failure of the resistance should not be judged merely by the outcome of one vote in the Congress. Throughout its career, the resistance was a dynamic body, in erratic progress past democratic milestones. But the common thread of the story was this: the rebel leadership looked only to the moment, treading only so far as seemed sufficient, rather than striving for the limits of the possible. The failure of the resistance was partial, not total; it was a failure born of ambiguity, where a noble clarity was needed.

In this ambiguity, the Nicaraguan Resistance was not alone. What can be said of them is even more abjectly true of the Sandinista Front. Nor is much optimism warranted over the victorious opposition's prospects of holding together long beyond the elections of February 1990. Much depends on the extraordinary character of Violeta Chamorro, but far more on that of her many advisors' many factions. If recent history is anything to go by, they are little better at harnessing personal ambition for the common good.

This depressing picture suggests that under the frustration of the democratic idea in Nicaragua lies a deeper disturbance. At each level in the heap, Peter must see Paul's gain as his own loss. At length, in his own quest for security and fulfillment, the individual reaches a stark choice between resignation or pandering to a ferocious addiction to power. He is thrown back on nothing but his own conscience, or lack thereof, and the sense of community is lost. These are the wages of a primitive nation, halfway to modernity, the worst half first. Nicaragua's wealth, culture, and tradition are just enough to divide, but not enough to bind her people in a common heritage.

A political culture built almost completely on patronage and punishment cannot fail but produce ugly results. One vice breeds another: tyranny—helplessness—ignorance and despair—the raw struggle for power—tyranny: one may fall into the bloody cycle at any point. If it is to be broken, it must be along the same lines. That so many Nicaraguans continue to try is a tribute to the resilience of liberal ideals. Surely the message is that there will always be some white-winged hope, beyond the solitude and futility that men feel when encircled by barbarism.

EDITOR'S NOTE: On June 25, 1990, the last of the contra commanders handed in their arms to President Violeta Chamorro under the auspices of the United Nations Demobilization Commission.

Appendix

Chronology of Events

1961	Carlos Fonseca Amador founds FSLN
1979	
July 19	Fall of Somoza dynasty
1980	
July	First armed resistance: Dimas takes over town of Quilali with MILPAS unit
	Bermudez begins to organize former national guardsmen
	Collapse of reconstruction junta
December	"Final Offensive" of guerrillas in El Salvador fails
1981	
January	Reagan administration begins
April	Bermudez begins to receive aid from Argentina
August	FDN chartered
	Assistant Secretary of State Enders offers U.S. acceptance of Sandinistas, based on restraint in military buildup
November	$19 million for contras approved by Congress

1982

April   War between Britain and Argentina

             Eden Pastora declares war on Sandinistas

August   First Boland Amendment passed, prohibiting use of U.S. funds for overthrowing the government of Nicaragua

1984

June   Congress ends aid to contras

November   Elections in Nicaragua: Cruz quits, Ortega elected

             Elections in United States: Reagan reelected

1985

June   Congress approves $27 million in "humanitarian aid"

             UNO is chartered by Cruz, Robelo, and Calero

1986

June   House approves $100 million, including military aid

November   Connection between Iranian arms sales and contras exposed

1987

March   Sandinistas fail to halt contra reinfiltration at Bocay

August   Arias plan adopted by Central American presidents

1988

February   Reagan's request for aid turned down by Congress

March   Truce signed at Sapoa between contras and Sandinistas

1989

February   Sandinistas agree to hold elections by February 1990

Notes

An attempt has been made to document as many of the reports in this work as possible. Most of the information is derived from conversations, the private records of different persons, and unpublished documents. A systematic effort was made, between November 1988 and January 1989, to obtain authoritative statements "for the record." Many of the remarks recorded derive nonetheless from the author's casual notes of conversations taken between 1986 and the present. In the notes, they are marked by the author's initials. Some persons quoted continue their involvement in public life; their names are not mentioned so that their accounts may be freely reported. The author has attempted to reproduce their statements faithfully and completely.

Many people have given generously of their time, energy, and memory to help make this book possible. To them the author is profoundly grateful.

Chapter 1

1. Pedro Joaquin Gonzalez ("Dimas") was born in Matagalpa in 1945 and was a small farmer. He joined the FSLN in 1972 and became leader of the Milicias Populares Anti-Somocistas (MILPAS). In July 1980, he took over Quilali to protest collectivization of the *campesinos* and the totalitarian swing of the regime. He was murdered by a Sandinista double agent in August 1981. A regional command of the resistance is named after him.

2. During the war against Somoza, the acronym MILPAS

had read Milicias Populares Anti-Somocistas instead of the present "Anti-Sandinistas."

3. Eden Pastora Gomez, known as "Commander Zero," was born in 1937 and founded the Sandino Revolutionary Front in 1959. He was a guerrilla in the Pancasan campaign (1967), led the capture of the National Palace in Managua (1978), was commander of the Southern Front (1979), and was vice minister of defense (1979–1980). Pastora was exiled in 1981.

4. Naturally most U.S. accounts tend to obscure this. See, for instance, Roy Gutman, *Banana Diplomacy* (New York: Simon and Schuster, 1988), which is probably the most useful account yet published. Its purpose is to explain the U.S. policy; this bias is enough to make it difficult to see things in their proper proportions. Gutman dutifully finds the hand of the United States behind every move, though often it is a hand that does not matter. For instance, the reader must read more than 100 pages of narrative before being amazed to learn that "the Argentines maintained their presence through 1984, and it took the CIA well into 1983 to gain effective control over events" (p. 107).

5. Bosco Matamoros, "Our Struggle" (UNO-FDN paper, 1987).

6. Bernard Mandeville, *An Inquiry into the Origins of Honour, and the Usefulness of Christianity in War*, 1732 ed., reprint (London: Frank Cass & Co. Ltd., 1972), 201.

Chapter 2

1. R. Pardo-Maurer (RPM), "Aide-memoire of Meeting with John Biehl at Department of State," March 23, 1987.

2. Arturo J. Cruz, born in 1923, was an organizer of the political struggle against Somoza and was jailed for a year in 1954. Cruz was president of the Central Bank of Nicaragua (1979–1980), a member of the Sandinista junta (May 1980–March 1981), ambassador to the United States (1981), and presidential candidate of the internal opposition (1984).

3. Fernando "El Negro" Chamorro Rappaccioli, born in 1932, was a hero in the struggle against Somoza. He led an assault on the National Guard barracks at Diriamba (1960). Chamorro was commander of the Southern Front with Eden Pastora (1977), was captured and jailed after a bazooka attack on Somoza's bunker (1978), and was ransomed by Pastora's capture of the Nicaraguan national assembly. He was exiled in 1981.

4. Alfredo Cesar Aguirre, born in 1951, is an economist and industrial engineer with an MBA from Stanford University. Manager of San Antonio Sugar Mill, one of the largest agroindustrial complexes in Central America, he joined the FSLN (1977) and was jailed after participation in military activities (1978). Cesar directed the drafting of the Program of the Government of National Reconstruction and was secretary of the governing junta (1979). He was exiled in 1982.

5. Alfonso Robelo Callejas, born in 1939, is a chemical engineer who graduated from Rensselaer Polytechnic Institute. He coordinated the earthquake relief effort (1972), was president of the Chamber of Commerce, and founded the Nicaraguan Democratic Movement (1978). He led strikes against Somoza. Robelo was a member of the first junta (1979) and president of the Democratic Coordinator of the internal opposition (1981). He was exiled in 1982.

6. See Robert E. Sanchez, *Contra Aid: A Brief Chronology*, report prepared for the Library of Congress, Congressional Research Service, Foreign Affairs and National Defense Division, March 10, 1988.

Military Aid to Nicaragua
(in millions of U.S. dollars)

Year	USSR (calendar year)	United States (fiscal year)
1980	10	–
1981	160	–
1982	140	19*
1983	250	29*
1984	370	24
1985	250	–
1986	550	–
1987	500	70
1988	515	–

*Reported covert appropriation.
Note: U.S. fiscal year runs from November to October of the following calendar year. Soviet figures are estimates. Figures include only official U.S. government aid.
Sources: U.S. Department of Defense; U.S. Library of Congress, Congressional Research Service, U.S. Department of State (ARA-CEN).

7. Pedro Joaquin Chamorro Barrios, Jr., born in 1951, graduated from McGill University, Montreal, Canada. He was coeditor of *La Prensa* (1981-1984) and political secretary of the Social Democratic Party (1983).

8. Adolfo Calero Portocarrero, born in 1931, was chairman of Milca (Coca Cola) bottling company. In 1959, he organized strikes against Somoza and, as Conservative representative in the Broad Opposition Front against Somoza, was jailed briefly (1978). Calero was political secretary of the Democratic Conservative Party and was exiled in 1982.

9. Arturo J. Cruz, Jr., "Apuntes Generales para una Nueva Estrategia," notes, 1984, p. 27.

10. RPM, personal recollection.

11. Bruce Cameron, "1985," unpublished notes, p. 2. Reported by courtesy of the writer.

12. RPM, record of conversation, November 1986.

13. RPM, record of conversation with three combatants of the Southern Front, November 1986.

14. RPM, record of conversation with a former resistance official, January 1989.

15. Represented in the UNO Assembly were the exiled Conservative (PCN), Social Democratic (MSDN), Social Christian (PSCN), and Independent Liberal (PLI) parties; the Nicaraguan Democratic Movement (MDN); the Nicaraguan Democratic Union (UDN); Workers' Democratic Solidarity; Committee of Nicaraguan Democratic Workers; Kus Indian Sut Asla Nicaragua ra (KISAN); Democratic Action; Nicaraguan Workers' and Peasants' Union; and Nicaraguan Private Sector in Exile.

16. RPM, record of conversation with Alfonso Robelo, January 1989.

17. Colonel Enrique Bermudez Varela, born in 1932, specialized in military engineering. He trained at Agulhas Negras Academy in Brazil, at Fort Leavenworth in Kansas, at the School of the Americas in the Panama Canal Zone, and at the Inter-American Defense College in Washington, D.C. He was a math instructor, executive director of Managua Traffic Police, and Military attaché, Nicaraguan mission to the United States (1976-1979).

18. President Ronald Reagan, letter to Rep. Dave McCurdy, July 11, 1985.

19. Ibid.

20. Cameron, "1985," p. 6.

21. Ibid.

22. *Congressional Record*, 100th Cong., 1st sess. (June 15, 1987), H4884.

23. Curtin Winsor, Jr., "Morality and Limited War: Nicaraguan Considerations" (no date).

24. I am indebted to the Japanese sociologist Maruyama Masuo for this concept.

25. See, for instance, Fuerza Democrática Nicaragüense (FDN), *Propuesta de paz*, January 13, 1983; letter from the FDN to the ministers of foreign relations of the Contadora Group countries, June 29, 1983; Unidad Nicaragüense de Reconciliación (UNIR), proposal, January 7, 1985.

26. RPM, record of conversation with Ambassador Francis McNeil, January 12, 1989.

27. See Constantine Menges, *Inside the National Security Council* (New York: Simon and Schuster, 1988).

28. Gutman, *Banana Diplomacy*, 322.

29. *Congressional Record*, 99th Cong., 2d sess. (August 11, 1986).

30. Aristides Sanchez, born in 1943, was a lawyer and cattle-rancher. A Liberal Party activist, he was exiled in 1980. He joined the 15th of September Legion (1981), was secretary general of the FDN (1983), and director of the FDN (1984).

31. RPM, record of conversations, November 1988.

32. Bosco Matamoros Hueck, born in 1945, studied in Rome and Bologna and had strong family and political ties to the Somoza government. He was Nicaraguan representative at the UN Food and Agriculture Organization (FAO) and joined the FDN in 1983.

33. Xavier Arguello Hurtado, born in 1952 in Caracas of exiled parents, was national coordinator of the MDN (1978). He participated in the Southern Front (1979) and served as secretary general of the Ministry of Culture (1979). He was director of the official government magazine *Nicarahuac* (1980-1984). He was exiled in 1984.

34. RPM, record of conversation with Xavier Arguello, November 20, 1988.

35. My own experience may be worth recounting to convey a

sense of the problems that plagued UNO as late as 1987. With the help of professors from several law faculties, I had outlined a proposal to restrict the use of antipersonnel mines. One of Calero's lieutenants arranged an interview for me with Calero, saying I should show my proposal to him.

In the room besides Calero were "Father" Dowling, an unidentified man who wore the rosette of the Knights of Malta, and Alvaro Rizo, a trustee of the FDN's fund-raising operation. The presence of these people was inauspicious. Dowling was a charlatan who posed as a Roman Catholic priest and later confessed to perjury before Congress. Rizo's reputation had been tarnished, among other things, by connections to Spitz Channel and a contra fund-raising dinner he had helped organize. The event managed to lose money even though President Reagan himself had attended and over $250,000 was said to have been raised.

Calero indicated approval of the proposal and appointed Rizo as my channel to him in order to develop it. This was in clear defiance of the institutionality of UNO and a typical example of the parallel structures that had hampered the organization. Rizo held no office in UNO. My line of communication to Calero should have proceeded through the Washington representative, Ernesto Palazio.

Even more unfortunate was that, after the meeting, Rizo drew me aside for another conversation. He said directly that Calero intended to remove "the people like Palazio," who were "in the way." New people would be needed in Washington. "A high salary" was offered if I cooperated. This I did not accept.

No more was heard of the project to restrict use of landmines. But a few weeks later, the Salvadoran guerrillas advanced an almost identical proposal that brought favorable coverage and reaped for them a welcome propaganda coup.

36. Robert W. Owen, confidential memorandum to Lt. Col. Oliver North, March 17, 1986, entered in the hearings of the Iran-Contra Committee as Exhibit RWO-13, p. 216.

37. Ibid.

38. Note from Robert McFarlane to John Poindexter, June 11, 1986, entered in the hearings of the Iran-Contra Committee as Exhibit 46D, p. 624.

39. Arturo J. Cruz, Jr., "Calero, el FDN y el Sur, despues del

documento de marzo y del documento de El Salvador en junio de 1985," notes, July 1985, p. 37.

40. RPM, record of conversation with Alfonso Robelo, January 1989.

41. RPM, record of conversation with Xavier Arguello, November 1988.

42. RPM, record of conversation with Alfonso Robelo, January 1988.

Chapter 3

1. The White House, "Report on Nicaragua" (mimeo.), November 6, 1985.

2. Robert W. Owen, memorandum to Lt. Col. Oliver North, November 26, 1985, entered in the hearings of the Iran-Contra Committee as Exhibit RWO-10.

3. See the *Congressional Record*, March 10, 1987, notes entered by Rep. Jerry Lewis (R-Ca.).

4. RPM, record of conversations with Hernan Castro Hernandez, adviser to Rafael Angel Calderon Fournier, January 1989.

5. Matamoros, "Our Struggle."

6. Dave McCurdy, "A Compromise on Nicaragua," *Washington Post*, March 14, 1986. Other quotations in paragraph from same source.

7. Bruce Cameron observes that the fundamental problem was that Cruz and Robelo felt that they could not hold on to that position "in the face of opposition from the Administration." Cameron, "1985," p. 16.

8. Peter T. Flaherty, "The Strategy Worked," mimeographed and circulated to contra activists, September 15, 1986.

9. See, for instance, "The Case for the Contras," *New Republic*, March 24, 1986.

10. RPM, personal recollection.

11. RPM, record of conversation with an aide to Senator Kassebaum, November 1988.

12. Leonardo Somarriba Gonzalez, born in 1938, is a civil engineer. He was former vice president of the Nicaraguan Chamber of Commerce and a manager of Esso in Nicaragua. He was

jailed for a year by the Sandinistas in 1980 for alleged conspiracy against the regime.

13. Carlos Ulvert Sanchez, born in 1945, trained as a chemist and agronomist and possesses an MBA from Harvard. A former Nicaraguan Central Bank officer, he left Nicaragua in 1979. He is affiliated with "El Negro" Chamorro.

14. U.S. Department of State, "Democratic Reforms and Support for a Peaceful Solution to the Conflict in Nicaragua," mimeographed, June 1986.

15. Unidad Nicaragüense Opositora (UNO), "Acuerdos Basicos," Miami, Florida, May 29, 1986.

16. Unidad Nicaragüense Opositora (UNO), "Alfonso Robelo Defines Strategy and Objectives of UNO," *Nicaragua Update*, Washington Office, January 31, 1987.

17. Cameron, "1985," p. 25.

18. E. Cody, "Contras' Leaders Again Divided by Rivalry between Politicians, Fighters," *Washington Post*, September 26, 1986. See also, J. LeMoyne, "4 Months after Pact, Contras' Leaders Clash," *New York Times*, September 26, 1986.

19. RPM, record of conversations with Alfonso Robelo, November 1988.

20. Secretaria de Divulgacion y Propaganda de la Alianza Revolucionaria Democrática (ARDE), *Toma del Rio San Juan*, mimeographed booklet, no date (probably 1986).

21. RPM, record of conversations with Adolfo Calero, November 1988.

22. Arturo J. Cruz, Jr., "Calero, el FDN y el Sur, despues del documento de marzo y del documento de El Salvador en junio de 1985," p. 37.

23. Robert W. Owen, "Southern Front," April 17, 1986, memorandum to Lt. Col. Oliver North, entered in the hearings of the Iran-Contra Committee as Exhibit RWO-7.

24. Ibid.

25. Michael J. Ledeen, *Perilous Statecraft* (New York: Scribner's, 1988), 57.

26. Owen, "Southern Front" (memorandum).

27. Lt. Col. Oliver North, "Private Blank Check," August 31, 1985, note to Adm. John Poindexter, entered in the hearings of the Iran-Contra Committee as Exhibit 46C.

28. Arturo J. Cruz, Jr., "Apuntes Generales para una Nueva Estrategia," notes, 1985, pp. 6–7.

Chapter 4

1. UNO, "Alfonso Robelo Defines Strategy."
2. Ibid.
3. Matamoros, "Our Struggle."
4. "Arturo Cruz's Choice," *Washington Post*, February 6, 1987.
5. RPM, record of conversation, January 15, 1989.
6. RPM, record of conversation with Arturo Cruz, Jr., January 1989.
7. See J. Preston, "Nicaraguan Rebel Alliance Shaky," *Washington Post*, January 29, 1987.
8. RPM, record of conversation with José Davila, December 1986.
9. Roberto Jiron, "Testimony," manuscript, June 10, 1987.
10. Ibid.
11. RPM, record of conversation with Bosco Matamoros, November 21, 1988.
12. RPM, record of conversation with Adolfo Calero, November 1988.
13. RPM, record of conversation with Arturo Cruz, Sr., November 9, 1988.
14. UNO, "Memorandum: Objectives," Washington Office, February 19, 1987.
15. Ibid.
16. Resistance Directorate press conference, National Press Club, Washington, D.C., August 5, 1987.
17. Arturo J. Cruz, "A mis compatriotas," speech, March 10, 1987.
18. RPM, record of conversations with Adolfo Calero, November 1988.
19. Arturo J. Cruz, "A mis compatriotas."
20. RPM, record of conversations with Adolfo Calero, November 1988.
21. RPM, "Aide-memoire of meeting with John Biehl at Department of State," March 23, 1987.
22. In public, the next day, Biehl would deny having said any such thing. Ibid.
23. UNO Secretariat for International Relations, "Observaciones sobre la propuesta de paz de San Jose," confidential white paper, March 1987.

24. See J. Gerth and S. Engleberg, "Cash for Contras Far Exceeds Sum They Had Sought," *New York Times*, April 8, 1987.

25. Senators W. S. Cohen, N. L. Kassebaum, W. B. Rudman, "A Policy on Nicaragua," *Washington Post*, April 6, 1987.

26. Commanders "Leonel," "Oscar," and "Navegante," "Comunicado de Talolinga," March 25, 1987.

27. Resistencia Nicaragüense, "Acta Patriotica de la Resistencia Nicaragüense," May 8, 1987.

28. RPM, record of conversation with Leonardo Somarriba, January 1989.

29. UNO-Washington Office, Press Release, March 4, 1987.

30. RPM, personal recollection.

31. Resistance Directorate press conference, National Press Club, Washington, D.C., August 5, 1987.

32. Resistencia Nicaragüense, "Declaration," San Salvador, August 21, 1987.

33. Resistencia Nicaragüense, "Communiqué," Los Angeles, August 27, 1987.

34. CID poll, as published in *La Nacion* (Costa Rica), December 29, 1987. See also, *Congressional Record*, March 10, 1987.

35. Coordinadora Democrática Nicaragüense, "Document," Caracas, December 4 and 5, 1987.

36. See James LeMoyne, "Sandinistas Warn Opposition Not to Push Too Far," *New York Times*, December 17, 1987.

37. *New York Times*, November 5, 1987.

38. "Nasty Choices on Nicaragua," *New York Times*, December 18, 1987.

39. RPM, record of conversation with José Sorzano, November 22, 1988.

Chapter 5

1. "The Contras Are Interested," *Washington Post*, January 2, 1988.

2. Rep. Dave McCurdy and 19 others, letter to the president of the United States, January 21, 1988.

3. Rep. Dave McCurdy, "We Would Bail Out on Peace with Aid to the Contras," *Los Angeles Times*, December 23, 1987.

4. Rep. Jim Slattery, letter to the Speaker of the U.S. House of Representatives, January 25, 1988.

5. RPM, record of meeting between Rep. Jim Slattery and directors of the Nicaraguan Resistance, February 1988.

6. Senator Sam Nunn and others, letter to the president of the United States, January 25, 1988.

7. RPM, record of conversation with a senior administration official [not Elliott Abrams], November 1988.

8. RPM, record of conversation with Rep. John Spratt, Jr., November 21, 1988.

9. Rep. Jim Wright and others, letter to the president of the United States, February 9, 1988.

10. Alfredo Cesar, letter of February 24, 1988.

11. RPM, "Aide-memoire of a meeting between Alfredo Cesar, Ernesto Palazio, and the House Democratic Deputy Whip Dr. Bonior," February 18, 1988.

12. Alfredo Cesar, letter of February 24, 1988.

13. RPM, record of conversation with José Sorzano, November 22, 1988.

14. RPM, record of meeting between a task force Democrat and directors of the Nicaraguan Resistance, March 1989.

15. RPM, record of conversations with Adolfo Calero, November 1988.

16. See Nicaraguan Resistance Educational Foundation, "White Paper on the Breakdown of Negotiations," Washington, D.C., June 1988.

17. RPM, record of conversation with Donald Castillo, November 27, 1988.

18. RPM, record of conversations with Adolfo Calero, November 1988.

19. RPM, record of conversations with Adolfo Calero, November 30, 1988.

20. RPM, record of conversation with Donald Castillo, November 27, 1988.

21. RPM, record of conversation with Bosco Matamoros, November 21, 1988.

22. Glenn Garvin, *Washington Times*, May 3, 1988.

23. RPM, record of conversations, November 1988.

24. RPM, record of conversation with Pedro Joaquin Chamorro, Jr., November 25, 1988.

25. RPM, record of conversation with Glenn Garvin, November 1988.

26. RPM, record of conversation with Aristides Sanchez, November 1988.

27. RPM, record of conversation, November 29, 1988.

28. Tirzo Moreno (nom de guerre "Rigoberto"), "A mis companeros y hermanos . . . ," undated letter (probably July 1988).

29. Eight commanders of the Nicaraguan Resistance, letter to the president of the United States, September 28, 1988. This letter was not answered.

30. RPM, record of conversations, November 1988.

31. Thomas P. Glakas (aide to Rep. Skelton), memorandum, August 11, 1988.

32. Ibid.

33. Ibid.

34. RPM, record of conversations, January 1989.

35. RPM, letter from a former resistance official, November 23, 1988.

36. RPM, record of a meeting between William Perry and resistance officials, November 1988.

Postscript

1. Freedom House Working Group on Central America, *Peace through Democracy*, October 1988.

2. Aristides Sanchez, Alfredo Cesar, Enrique Bermudez, "1989: Estrategia de la RN," memorandum to the U.S. government, November 17, 1988.

Index

Abrams, Elliott, 32, 34–35, 58, 78, 102, 125
Air power, 74
Alianza Revolucionaria Democrática (ARDE), 20, 63
Andres Perez, Carlos, 42, 122, 126
Argentina, 2, 3
Arguello, Xavier, 39, 139n.33
Arias, Oscar, 48–49, 80–81, 89
Arias plan, 75, 80–83; Bush administration and, 125–126; Sandinista compliance with, 89–91, 94, 97, 118

Bermudez, Enrique, 2, 24, 138n.17; ambiguous commands of, 11; Calero and, 84; contra mutiny, 110–115; dependence on U.S. aid, 90; new contra directorate and, 121–122; opposition to UNO, 43; Regional Commanders' Council and, 61–62; Sapoa agreement and, 107–108; Southern Front and, 64
Biehl, John, 80–81
Bipartisan coalition, 118

Bloque Opositor del Sur (BOS), 21, 42–45, 63–67, 84
Boland Amendment, 28
Borge, Tomás, 12, 31, 118–119
BOS. *See* Bloque Opositor del Sur
Bush administration, 123–127

Calero, Adolfo, 14, 24, 138n.8; contra mutiny and, 110, 114; Cruz and, 23, 31–35, 75, 80; Declaration of San Jose and, 17; fund raising, 86; Iran-contra scandal and, 47; negotiation policy and, 33–35; new contra directorate and, 121; nonlethal aid package and, 100; Regional Commanders' Council and, 61–62; Republican divisions and, 89; resignation of, 75, 78; Sapoa agreement and, 105–108; Southern Front and, 64–65; UNO authority, 35–44, 57, 60, 140n.35; weakening position of, 75–76, 83–84
Calero, Mario, 41
Cameron, Bruce, 17–18, 27–28
Campesinos, 12, 24, 49

147

Carter administration, 4

Cease-fire enclaves, 105, 106

Cease-fire negotiations, 90, 97, 105–108

Central Intelligence Agency (CIA), 29; BOS and, 42; Congress and, 5, 7, 29, 36, 103; contra mutiny and, 113, 114; Pastora and, 2–3, 66, 69; shortcomings of, 5; Southern Front and, 65, 68, 76

Cesar, Alfredo, 13, 14, 20, 130, 137n.4; bipartisan aid proposal and, 120; BOS-UNO merger and, 84; contra mutiny and, 110–115; Cruz and, 21; humanitarian aid proposal, 90–91; independence of, 42; new contra directorate and, 121–122; nonlethal aid proposal and, 100–102; Republican divisions and, 89; Sapoa accord and, 106–108; Southern Front and, 63–65, 67

Chamorro, Fernando "El Negro", 13, 63–65, 67–69, 76, 136n.3

Chamorro, Pedro Joaquin, 14, 83, 112–115, 121, 138n.7

Chamorro, Violeta, 126, 127, 131

Channel, Carl, 86

CIA. See Central Intelligence Agency

Clarridge, Dewey, 69

Cohen, William S., 56–57, 82–83

Congress. See U.S. Congress

Contadora process, 32–35, 48, 51

Contras: achievements of, 128; appeal to President Reagan, 117; axis of leadership, 38; Bush election and, 123–124; CIA mistakes and, 5, 7; confusion of, 107–110; congressional balance of power and, 17–19; demoralization of, 115–118; disunity of, 8–9; political initiative, 92–95; Latin American support for, 2–3, 48–49; leadership failures, 129–131;

lobby for nonlethal aid, 100–103; military setbacks, 49–50, 105; military successes, 74, 94–95; mutiny of, 110–115; Nicaraguan elections and, 127; 1985 political strategy, 15–16; 1987 strategy, 73–74; 1988 optimism, 96; number of forces, 74; personal differences, 19–22; Republican divisions and, 100; Sapoa agreement and, 104–106; Southern Front, 62–70, 83; tacit bargain with Congress, 91. See also Nicaraguan Democratic Force; United Nicaraguan Opposition; specific organizations, persons

Costa Rica, 48–49, 52, 68, 118

Cruz, Arturo, 13–15, 30–31, 136n.1; Calero vs., 23, 31–35, 75, 80; Cesar and, 21; contra reform and, 23; Declaration of San Jose and, 17–18; FDN and, 25, 38, 61–62; lack of influence, 42–44; leadership failure, 129–130; military aid politics and, 53; negotiation policy and, 33–35; resignation of, 45, 46, 75, 78–80; UNO reform efforts, 44–45, 55–60, 78–80; U.S. Congress and, 55–56

Cruz, Arturo, Jr., 14–15, 41–42, 65

Cuba, 66

Declaration of San Jose, 17–18

Democratic Coordinator, 13–14, 23, 93

Democratization: Arias plan, 81; contra reform and, 23; Sandinista opposition to, 48

Democrats (U.S.), 14–15; Declaration of San Jose and, 17; nonlethal aid proposal, 100–104; swing voters, 18–19, 26–28, 51–55, 97–99. See also U.S. Congress

"Dimas," 2, 135n.1

Dole, Robert, 57, 88, 119–120
Dominican Republic, 120
Duarte, José Napoleón, 18, 90

Ejército Popular Sandinista (EPS), 49, 50
Elections, 119, 123, 126–127
El Salvador, 17–18, 81
Esquipulas agreement, 89, 93. *See also* Arias plan
Exiles, 41

FDN. *See* Nicaraguan Democratic Force
Ferch, John, 34–35
"Fernando," 110–113, 116
Financial resources, control of, 78–79
Flaherty, Peter, 54
FODENIC, 76
Freedom Fighter Supply Fund, 86
Freedom House, 125
Frente Sandinista de Liberación Nacional (FSLN). *See* Sandinista National Liberation Front
FSLN. *See* Sandinista National Liberation Front
Fuerza Democrática Nicaragüense (FDN). *See* Nicaraguan Democratic Force
Fund raising, 36, 41, 86, 123

Gonzalez, Pedro Joaquin ("Dimas"), 135n.1
Gorbachev, Mikhail, 97

Herdocia, Gustavo, 76
Honduras, 48, 52; Arias plan and, 81; contra mutiny and, 111–113; contra refugees in, 76, 118; contra retreat to, 49, 108; Nicaraguan Resistance and, 85; Sandinista incursion, 105
Humanitarian aid, 27, 28–29, 37; bipartisan compromise, 51–55; Bush administration and, 127; contra proposal, 90–91; Democrat proposal for, 100–103; new bipartisan proposal, 119–120; short-term resolutions, 91; Sapoa agreement and, 106

Internal opposition: armed resistance and, 13–17; demands for new regime, 93; Sandinista repression of, 118–119
Iran-contra affair, 47, 71, 72, 87

Kassebaum, Nancy, 56–57, 82–83
Kemp, Jack, 88, 89, 91

Legion, 15th of September, 2

McCurdy, Dave, 26, 51–55, 97
McFarlane, Robert, 41
Managua I talks, 107
Managua II talks, 108
Manzanillo talks, 8–9, 26
Matamoros, Bosco, 38–39, 74, 77, 109
May Reforms, 46, 58–61
Meese, Edwin, 47
Milicias Populares Anti-Sandinistas (MILPAS), 2
Military aid, 26; contra lobbying, 100–103; cutoff, 18, 36, 104; Declaration of San Jose and, 18; May Reforms and, 46, 60–61; nonlethal bipartisan compromise, 51–55; Sandinista concessions and, 97–99; secret supplies, 28–29, 36–37; State Department and, 34–35
Military engagements: Bocay region, 74, 105; contra successes, 74, 94–95; Sandinista successes, 49–50, 105
MILPAS (Milicias Populares Anti-Sandinistas), 2
Miskito Indians, 22, 55

Monge, Luis Alberto, 48
Motley, Langhorne, 34

Negroponte, John, 34
Nicaraguan Democratic Force
    (FDN), 2, 8, 24–25; Calero and,
    36; early strategy, 11; internal
    opposition and, 13–17; military
    setbacks, 49–50; misassessment
    of Sandinistas by, 9–10; 1987
    strategy, 74; number of forces,
    63; political wing of, 76; predom-
    inance in UNO, 37–41; refugee
    settlements and, 76; Regional
    Commanders' Council, 61; rural-
    based strategy, 12; Southern
    Front and, 63–65; UNO misgiv-
    ings, 25, 38, 42; UNO reforms
    and, 58–60. See also Contras;
    United Nicaraguan Opposition;
    specific persons
Nicaraguan Democratic Union
    (UDN), 2
Nicaraguan Resistance: chartered,
    84–86; confusion after Sapoa
    agreements, 107–110; contra mu-
    tiny, 110–115; end of U.S. aid to,
    104; new directorate of, 120–121.
    See also Contras
Nicaraguan Resistance fund, 123
Nonlethal aid. See Humanitarian
    aid
North, Oliver, 26–27, 32, 36, 40–
    41, 45, 48, 63–65, 68

O'Neill, Thomas "Tip", 54
Obando y Bravo, Miguel Cardinal,
    94, 104
Ortega, Daniel: accepts Arias plan,
    97; allows elections, 126; contra
    military power and, 71; internal
    opposition vs., 93–94; negotiates
    with contras, 105; popular sup-
    port for, 12–13; trip to Moscow,
    18, 26, 33

Ortega, Humberto, 92, 105
Owen, Robert, 40–41, 65, 67, 68

Palazio, Ernesto, 86
Pastora, Eden, 2, 13, 42, 136n.3;
    assassination attempt, 66–67;
    CIA and, 2–3, 66, 69; Southern
    Front and, 65–67, 69; State De-
    partment and, 42; UNO and, 20,
    21–22
Patriotic Covenant, 85
Poindexter, John, 40, 57
Political opposition. See Internal
    opposition
Psychological warfare, 92

Reagan, Ronald: contra dissident
    appeal to, 117; "founding fa-
    thers" speech, 29; identification
    with contras, 54
Reagan administration: congres-
    sional backlash against, 7; con-
    tra group unification and, 8–9;
    contra reform and, 57; Demo-
    cratic opposition, 17; early San-
    dinista policy, 3–5; El Salvador
    policy, 17–18; Iran-contra affair,
    71, 72; negotiation policy divi-
    sions, 32–35; Sandinista negotia-
    tions, 26–28; sends troops to
    Honduras, 105; two-track policy,
    8, 16, 22, 99; UNO leadership di-
    visions and, 31–35
Reagan-Wright plan, 87–89
Refugees, 76, 118
Religious freedom, 24
Republicans: Calero-Cesar rivalry
    and, 89; contra coalition, 51; in-
    ternal divisions, 89, 100; nonle-
    thal aid proposal, 103–104. See
    also U.S. Congress
"Rigoberto," 110, 111, 116–117
Rivas, Luis "Wicho", 77
Robelo, Alfonso, 13, 14, 23, 137n.5;
    congressional politics and, 56;

Declaration of San Jose and, 17; FDN and, 25, 38, 61–62; military aid politics, 53; 1987 contra strategy, 73, 79; UNO leadership, 21; UNO reform efforts, 44–45, 55–60

Rudman, Warren, 56–57, 82–83

Sanchez, Aristides, 38, 84, 107, 113–115, 139n.30

Sandinista National Liberation Front (FSLN): agrees to indirect mediation, 94; Arias plan and, 89–91, 94, 97–99; diplomatic solutions and, 47–50; early resistance to, 2; FDN misassessment of, 9–10; final defeat of, 128; internal support for, 4; internal opposition vs., 93–94; intransigence of, 106–108; military setbacks, 74, 94–95; military successes, 49–50, 105; new diplomatic initiative, 114; popular disillusionment, 12; Sapoa agreement and, 104–106; strengths of, 10; U.S. aid politics and, 50, 104; U.S. talks with, 26–28, 32–33; weaponry, 74

Sapoa agreement, 104–110

Saudi Arabia, 36

Shultz, George, 34, 91

Slattery, Jim, 97–98

Somarriba, Leonardo, 58, 75

Southern Front, 62–70, 76, 83. See also Bloque Opositor del Sur

Soviet Union, 97

Strategic Command of the Sandinista Army (EPS), 49

Swing Democrats, 18–19, 26–28, 51–55, 97–99

"Toño," 110, 111

Two-track policy, 8, 16, 22, 99

Ulvert, Carlos, 58, 68–69, 142n.13

Union Democrática Nicaragüense (UDN), 2

United Nicaraguan Opposition (UNO), 5; Arias plan and, 81–82; BOS merger, 84; Calero authority, 35–44, 57, 60, 140n.35; congressional politics and, 55–57; contra reform and, 22–23; Cruz reform agenda, 44–45; Cruz resignation, 75, 78–80; FDN misgivings, 25; FDN predominance, 37–41; lack of respect for, 41–42; leadership problems, 20–21, 75–80, 83–84; May Reforms, 58–60; Nicaraguan Resistance chartered, 84–86; 1987 reform agenda, 78–80; press secretary, 39; Southern Front, 63–65, 76, 83; White House divisions and, 31–35

U.S. government, early Sandinista policy, 4–5. See also Reagan administration; U.S. Congress

UNO. See United Nicaraguan Opposition

Urban resistance, 11–12

U.S. Congress: CIA and, 5, 7, 29, 36, 103; contra coalition, 51; contra reform and, 26–30, 46, 55–57, 60; humanitarian aid compromise, 28–29; military aid cutoff, 18; moderates in, 43; new bipartisan initiative, 119–120; nonlethal aid compromise, 51–55, 100–104; Reagan-Wright plan, 87–89; swing voters, 18–19, 26–28, 51–55, 97–99; tacit bargain with, 91

U.S. State Department, 33–35

Venezuela, 42

Weaponry, 49, 74

Winsor, Curtin, 29, 34

Wright, Jim, 87–89, 122